Sew Flower Quilts & Gifts

30 patchwork, quilting and appliqué projects using fabric scraps

Atsuko Matsuyama

First published in Great Britain 2017

Search Press Limited
Wellwood, North Farm Road,
Tunbridge Wells, Kent, TN2 3DR

Reprinted 2017

English language rights, translation & production by Zakka Workshop
English Editors: Lindsay Fair and Kristyne Czepuryk
Translation: Kyoko Matthews

Suppliers
If you have any difficulty obtaining any of the materials and equipment
mentioned in this book, please visit the Search Press website.
www.searchpress.com

ISBN: 978-1-78221-489-2

Printed in China
10 9 8 7 6 5 4 3 2

Contents

Triangle Baby Quilt

I designed this quilt for expectant mothers looking for a relaxing project to work on while awaiting the arrival of their bundles of joy. The pink stripes and borders used here work well for a girl, while blue or yellow would be great for a baby boy.

Instructions on page 38

Flowers & Birds Baby Quilt

Considering that this quilt might be one of the things a baby sees in the precious first moments of life, I was inspired to use bright, beautiful colors. This quilt makes a wonderful present for a baby shower . . . any baby who receives it is sure to grow up to be a nature lover!

Instructions on page 40

Patchwork Pencil Case & Patchwork Scissor Caddy

This ladylike pencil case makes a great home for your favorite marking pens, seam gauges, and thimbles. The coordinating scissor caddy is the perfect size for storing a pair of thread clips.

Instructions on pages 42 and 45

Dresden Plate

Log Cabin

Shoofly

Pretty Pin Cushions

Breathe new life into old scraps with these adorable little pin cushions. Choose from a Dresden plate, log cabin, or shoofly motif. Lace and pompoms add a special touch!

Instructions on pages 47, 49, and 51

Sewing Kit

This one-of-a-kind sewing kit is the perfect home for your favorite quilting tools and notions. The inside of the kit contains specially designed storage solutions for your scissors, rulers, pens, spools, thimbles, and pins, while the outside is decorated with a fun sewing-inspired motif.

Instructions on page 53

Yoyo Lanyards

Decorate store-bought lanyards with brightly printed yoyos, then embellish with sequins, beads, and lace flowers to create a gorgeous ID card holder, inspired by a Hawaiian lei.

Instructions on page 62

Floral Corsage Bracelet

Construct a three-dimensional floral corsage using fabric, fusible web, and wool felt balls. This scrap-friendly project makes a festive addition to any outfit!

Instructions on page 64

Lunch Tote, Snack Satchel, & Lunch Mat

Whether you're enjoying a picnic in the park or you're on your lunch break, this three-piece set will add a helping of cheer to your midday meal. The Lunch Tote and Snack Satchel feature drawstring closures to keep your food safe and secure, while the Lunch Mat rolls up for easy transport.

Instructions on pages 66, 70, and 72

3-D Appliqué Mini Purse

This sweet little project makes an adorable purse for a little girl...it's just large enough to store all of her little treasures. Don't be intimidated by the appliqué—the three-dimensional flowers are actually quite simple to make.

Instructions on page 105

Patchwork Placemats

These simple placemats are a quick and easy way to brighten up your kitchen. Just piece five rectangles together, quilt, then embellish with lace appliqués.

Instructions on page 74

Heart Tea Pot Cozy & Mat

Designed for tea lovers, the heart-themed set shown on the opposite page elevates everyday teatime to a special occasion worthy of celebration. Give this adorable set as a heartfelt housewarming gift or make it yourself to decorate your kitchen on Valentine's Day.

Instructions on pages 76 and 79

Strawberry Spring Mini Quilt

Featuring basic patchwork techniques, appliqué motifs, and embroidery stitches, this wall hanging makes an ideal first project for quilting beginners. In fact, step-by-step photos for this project are included in the Technique Guide on pages 29–34. Once you master these basic techniques, you'll be ready to tackle any of the projects in this book.

Instructions on page 81

Sweet Summertime Mini Quilt

I love a good cherry motif just as much as I love strawberries. For this miniature wall hanging. I used a dot print for the background fabrics and a curved border to complement the round silhouette of the appliquéd cherries.

Instructions on page 83

Autumn Symphony Wall Hanging

Bursting with wonderful sights and sounds, autumn is one of my favorite seasons:
mushrooms sprout from the forest floor and birds hunt for nuts. The scallop border
on this wall hanging was inspired by fallen leaves.

Instructions on page 85

Winter Wonderland Wall Hanging

I know that fir trees are more traditional at Christmas, but I couldn't help decorating this tree with apples! And this snowman looks quite happy with the results!

Instructions on page 87

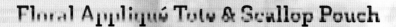

Floral Appliqué Tote & Scallop Pouch

This coordinating set celebrates the arrival of spring. I love combining polka dots, plaids, and prints within the same project. The geometric designs complement the fruit and flower prints. The Scallop Pouch is featured in the Technique Guide, which includes step-by-step photos for basic bag making techniques, such as finishing seam allowances and installing a zipper.

Instructions on pages 89 and 93

Hexagon Zip Pouch

I used vintage feedsack fabrics to add a pop of color to this hexie pouch. Looking at these vibrant, cheerful colors, it's hard to believe that some of these fabrics may be more than 80 years old!

Instructions on page 95

Happy Flower Clutch

This pouch was designed specifically for those of you who don't enjoy installing zippers. Instead of a zipper, this clutch features a feminine scalloped flap and a magnetic snap. Can you spot the tiny butterfly appliqué?

Instructions on page 97

Lovely Vines Quilt

I chose to use simple appliqué and patchwork motifs for this quilt in order to showcase the beautiful colors and patterns of the fabric. The green and white color scheme provides a soothing backdrop for the bold and bright prints.

Instructions on page 115

Windmill Passport Case

This passport case is so bright and cheerful that it will be impossible to accidentally leave behind when traveling! I used a variety of floral patterns, including both small and large prints. Enjoy experimenting with color and scale while selecting fabrics for this design.

Instructions on page 100

Big Sister Tote & Little Sister Tote

These quick and easy tote bags are a breeze to make: Use pre-quilted fabric, then embellish with a hint of patchwork. The Big Sister Tote is great for sleepovers, while the Little Sister Tote is the perfect size for ballet shoes.

Instructions on pages 110 and 113

Happy Flower Quilt Sampler

This quilt was inspired by my favorite color, which is pink, as you may have already guessed. Although this quilt might look intimidating, it's actually suitable for quilters of all levels because it's composed of traditional patchwork and appliqué blocks. I've included photos for some of my favorite blocks on pages 26–27. You can use these designs individually or combine them to create this fun quilt.

Instructions on page 118

Patchwork Block Close-Ups from the Happy Flower Quilt Sampler

Old Maid's Puzzle

LeMoyne Star

Eight Point Star

Hearts

Honey Bee

Postage Stamp Basket

Bow Tie

Road to Oklahoma

Spools

Appliqué Block Close-Ups from the Happy Flower Quilt Sampler

Lovebird

Daisy

Pansy

Cherries

Strawberry

Morning Glory

Tulips

Apple

Four-Leaf Clover

Tools & Materials

Patchwork and Quilting

1. Piecing thread
2. Quilting thread
3. Basting thread
4. Needles
5. Needle threader
6. Pins
7. Paperweight
8. Cutting mat
9. Large ruler
10. Leather thimble
11. Metal thimble
12. Rubber thimble
13. Rotary cutter
14. Tracing wheel
15. Pen-style glue
16. Marking pen
17. Paper scissors
18. Fabric scissors
19. Thread clips
20. Patchwork board
21. Small ruler

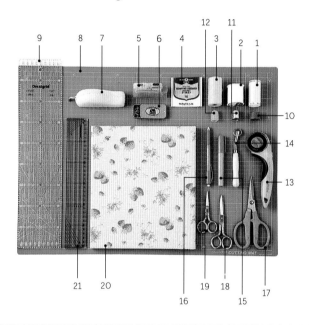

Applique and Embroidery

1. Beads
2. Sequins
3. Lace flowers
4. Embroidery needles
5. Freezer paper
6. Embroidery thread
7. Appliqué thread

Technique Guide

How to Make a Quilt

The following guide contains my favorite techniques for making a quilt from start to finish, including making templates, piecing, appliquéing, embroidering, quilting, and binding. This guide uses the Strawberry Spring Mini Quilt on page 16 as an example, but these techniques are used for a variety projects throughout the book. Mastering these techniques will help you create a beautifully finished quilt.

Gather Your Materials

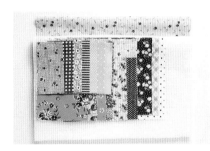

1. Select your fabrics for the quilt top, as well as the backing and binding. Gather your batting and other tools and materials you'll need to create the quilt.

Make the Templates

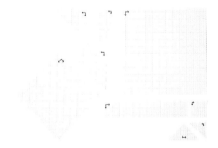

2. Trace the templates you'll need from the pattern sheet. You may want to make card stock templates, which are more durable than paper. Don't forget to mark the grainlines.

Piecing

3. Align the template with the wrong side of the fabric. Trace the template onto the fabric. Draw ¼in (5mm) seam allowance around all edges, then cut out the fabric pieces.

5. Pin two pieces with right sides together. When working with right triangles, it's important to remember that the longest side falls on the bias, so it tends to stretch—use pins at both ends and the center.

4. Insert the needle one stitch before the seam allowance mark. Make one backstitch in the seam allowance, then sew along the lines using running stitch.

6. At the end of the seam, make one backstitch in the seam allowance.

7. Fold the seam allowance toward the darker fabric. Crease using your fingernails.

8. Unfold, then finger press the seam open from the right side.

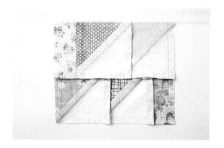

9. Use this process to sew pieces together in rows, then sew the rows together. Fold seam allowances as shown, then press with the iron.

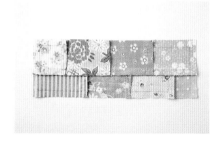

10. Follow the same process to sew the rectangular pieces together.

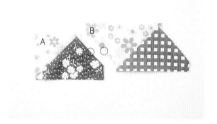

11. To make the bottom border, sew the triangular pieces together in sets. Make two A sets and four B sets.

12. To make the triangular bottom border, align the ○ marks (see previous step) and sew.

Appliqué & Embroidery

13. Trace the appliqué pieces onto the rough side of the freezer paper, then cut out.

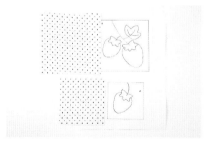

14. Trace the appliqué motifs onto the pieces of background fabric.

15. Align each piece of freezer paper from step 13 on the right side of the appliqué fabric (align the freezer paper with the smooth side down). Use an iron to adhere the freezer paper to the fabric.

16. Cut out the appliqué fabric, leaving ¼in (7mm) seam allowance. Glue the appliqué fabric to the background fabric using pen-style glue.

17. Thread an appliqué needle with a piece of thread in the same color as the fabric. Insert the needle through the appliqué fabric and draw it out close to the freezer paper.

18. Hemstitch the appliqué fabric to the background fabric, folding the seam allowance under as you work.

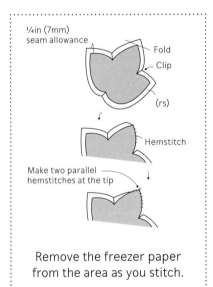

19. Continue appliquéing, working from the bottom layer to the top.

20. Cut a 19 ¾in (50cm) piece of embroidery floss. Separate two strands to use for embroidery.

21. Realign the two strands of floss. This process will prevent the floss from tangling as you work.

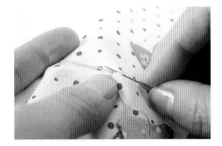

22. Embroider as indicated on the templates. When outline stitching, the key is to draw the needle out at the same point it was inserted.

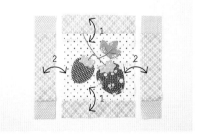

23. After the double strawberry block has been appliquéd and embroidered, sew the remaining pieces to the block following numerical order indicated above.

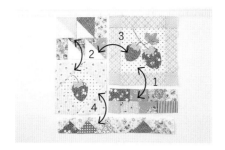

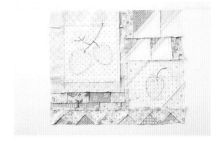

24. After the single strawberry block has been appliquéd and embroidered, sew the remaining pieces to the block following numerical order indicated above.

25. To assemble the top, sew the blocks together following numerical order indicated above.

26. Press the seam allowances as shown.

Quilting

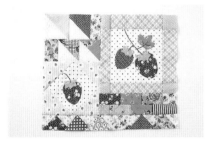

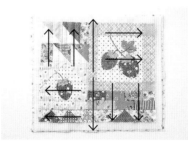

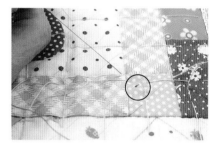

27. Mark the quilting lines on the quilt top.

28. Layer the top, batting, and backing. Starting from the center and working outward, smooth out to remove the air trapped between the layers. Baste the layers together as shown by the arrows, using lines spaced about 1 ¼in (3cm) apart.

29. Make a knot at the end of your quilting thread. Insert the needle into the quilt a bit away from where you'd like to make your first stitch. Draw the needle out one stitch ahead of where you'd like to make your first stitch.

30. Pull the thread taut to bring the knot through the quilt top and hide it inside the batting. Make two backstitches, then quilt with the running stitch. When you reach the end, make one backstitch. Hide the knot inside the batting.

31. Once the quilting is complete, remove the basting stitches. Baste around the edge of the quilt along the finishing lines. Trim the excess batting and backing so they are even with the quilt top.

Binding

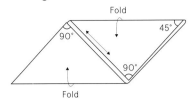

32. Fold the fabric as shown.

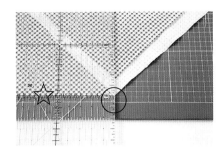

33. The ☆ fold should be parallel to the edge of the cutting mat. Align the ruler as indicated by the ○ and cut.

34. Rotate the board 180°. Cut 1 ½in (3.5cm) wide bias strips.

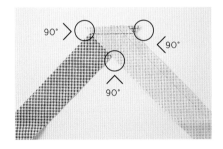

35. Align two bias strips with right sides together so that the three ○s form 90° angles. Backstitch together.

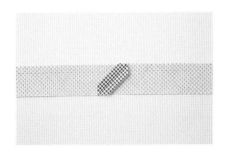

36. Press the seam allowance open and trim the excess fabric.

37. Align the bias strip and the quilt with right sides together. Sew using ¼in (5mm) seam allowance. When you reach the corner, make a knot and cut the thread. Fold the bias strip back at a 45° angle.

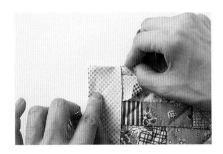

38. Fold the bias strip back down so it is even with the edge of the quilt. Make a backstitch through all layers at the corner, then continue sewing along the other side of the quilt.

39. Use this process to bind the entire quilt. When you reach the end, trim the bias strip so that it overlaps with the beginning ¼in (7mm). Layer the bias strips and sew together.

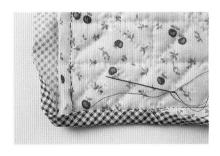

40. Wrap the binding to the back of the quilt and hemstitch to the backing.

41. When you reach the corner, fold the binding at a 45° angle using the needle tip.

42. Hemstitch the fold in place.

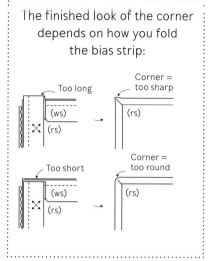

The finished look of the corner depends on how you fold the bias strip:

Too long

(ws)

(rs)

Corner = too sharp

(rs)

Too short

(ws)

(rs)

Corner = too round

(rs)

43. Use pins to hold the binding in place as you hemstitch.

44. Finished view of 45° angle corners.

45. Attach lace flowers, sequins, and beads.

46. Completed view of the quilt.

How to Make a Pouch

The following guide illustrates the techniques used to make a pouch from start to finish, including installing a zipper and finishing the seam allowances. This guide uses the Scallop Pouch on page 20 as an example, but these techniques are used for a variety of other pouch and bag projects throughout the book.

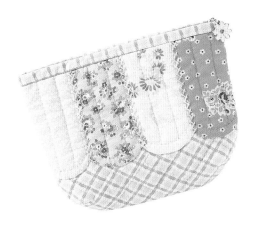

Gather Your Materials

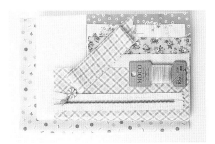

1. Select your fabrics for the pouch and gather your batting, zipper, and embroidery floss.

Make the Body

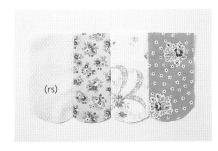

2. Use the templates provided to cut the scallop pieces out of fabric. Sew the scallop pieces together, stopping at the end of seam marks.

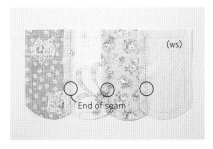

3. Press the seam allowances to one side.

4. Running stitch in the curved seam allowances, then pull the thread tails to gather the fabric around the template. Press to secure the shape.

5. Apply glue to the curved seam allowances.

6. Glue the patchwork pieces to the pouch lower front following placement indicated on the template.

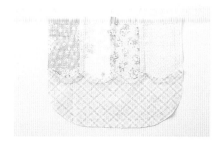

7. The scallop pieces have been glued to the lower front. Next, appliqué the scallops to the lower front to complete the front. Then trim away the excess fabric from the lower piece along the seam allowance.

Mark embroidery placement

8. Layer the front, batting and lining. Quilt, then use a tracing wheel to mark the embroidery placement.

9. Embroider as indicated on the template. Use a paperweight to hold the fabric flat while you work.

10. Completed view of the quilted and embroidered front. Sew the patchwork pieces together to create the back. Layer the back, batting, and lining and quilt.

11. Sew the darts in both the front and back. Align the front and back with right sides together and sew, leaving the pouch top open. (**Note:** The darts should be folded in opposite directions on the front and back.)

12. Trim the batting from the seam allowances.

Install the Zipper

13. Trim the seam allowances, except for one lining layer. The lining seam allowance should be at least ⅝in (1.5cm).

14. Wrap the untrimmed lining seam allowance around the others, tucking the raw edge under. Hemstitch in place to finish the seam.

15. Bind the pouch opening using the bias tape.

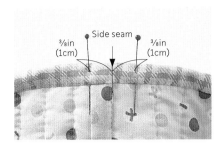

16. Insert pins ⅜in (1cm) from each side seam.

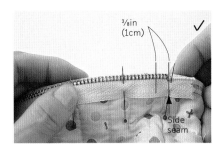

17. Pin the zipper to the pouch lining so that the teeth start ⅜in (1cm) from the side seam and are aligned with the binding edge.

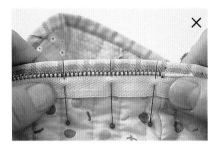

Make sure the teeth are aligned with the binding edge. You do not want the teeth positioned beneath the binding edge, as pictured here.

Nor do you want the zipper tape visible above the binding edge, as pictured here.

18. Backstitch the zipper to the binding, making sure the stitches are not visible on the outside of the pouch.

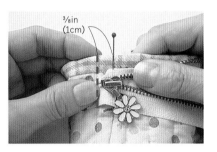

19. You should finish sewing ⅜in (1cm) from the other side seam.

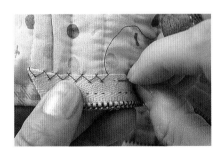

20. Follow the same process to attach the other side of the zipper. Fold short zipper ends under and catch stitch to sew the zipper to the lining.

21. Continue catch stitching to attach the other side of the zipper.

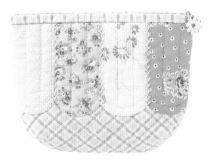

22. Completed view of the pouch.

Triangle Baby Quilt

Shown on page 4

Materials

- **Patchwork fabric:** Nine assorted fat eighths

- **Sashing/binding fabric:** 1 ⅛yd (1.1m) of light pink fabric

- **Border fabric:** ⅝yd (0.6m) of pink plaid fabric

- **Backing fabric:** 1 ⅓yd (1.3m) of fabric

- **Batting:** 43 ¼ x 45 ¼in (110 x 115cm)

Layout Diagram

Diagram shows finished measurements

Sew using ¼in (7mm) seam allowance, unless otherwise noted.

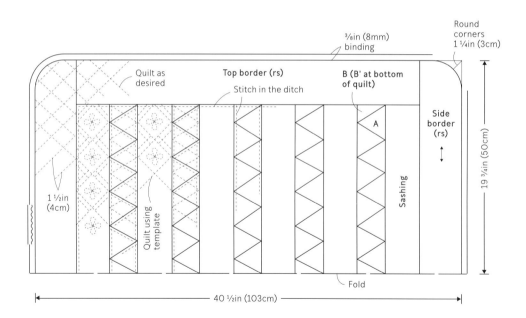

Cutting Instructions

Trace and cut out the templates on Pattern Sheet A. Cut out the following fabric pieces, adding ¼in (7mm) seam allowance:

Assorted fat eighths:
- 95 A pieces
- 5 B pieces
- 5 B' pieces

Cut out the following pieces, which do not have templates, according to the measurements below (these measurements include seam allowance):

Sashing/binding fabric:
- Sashings (cut 6): 3 ⅝ x 32in (9.4 x 81.4cm)
- Binding: 4 ½ yds (4.2m) of 1 ½in (3.5cm) wide single fold bias binding

Border fabric:
- Borders (cut 4): 4 ½in x WOF (11.4in x WOF)

Construction Steps

1. To make one pieced row of triangles, sew 19 A pieces together. Add one B to one end of the row and one B' to the other (refer to Figure 1).

2. Make five pieced rows.

3. To make the quilt top, sew the sashings and pieced rows together in an alternating pattern. Refer to Figure 2 and the diagram on page 38.

4. To add the top and bottom borders, measure the width of the pieced panel at the top, middle, and bottom. Calculate the average width, then add ½in (1.4cm) for seam allowance. Trim the top and bottom borders to that measurement. Pin and sew the borders to the pieced panel.

5. To add the side borders, measure the height of the quilt (including the top and bottom borders) at both sides and the middle. Calculate the average height, then add ½in (1.4cm) for seam allowance. Trim the side borders to that measurement. Pin and sew the borders to the quilt.

6. Layer the top, batting, and backing. Quilt as shown in the diagram on page 38. Use the template on Pattern Sheet A to quilt the sashings.

7. Make a mark 1 ¼in (3cm) from each corner. Connect the adjacent marks with a curved line. Trim along the curves to created rounded corners.

8. Bind the quilt (refer to pages 33–34).

Figure 1: Make the Pieced Row

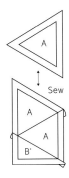

Figure 2: Sew the Sashings and Pieced Rows Together

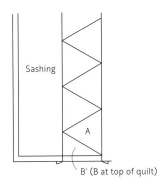

Flowers & Birds Baby Quilt

Shown on page 5

Layout Diagram

Diagram shows finished measurements

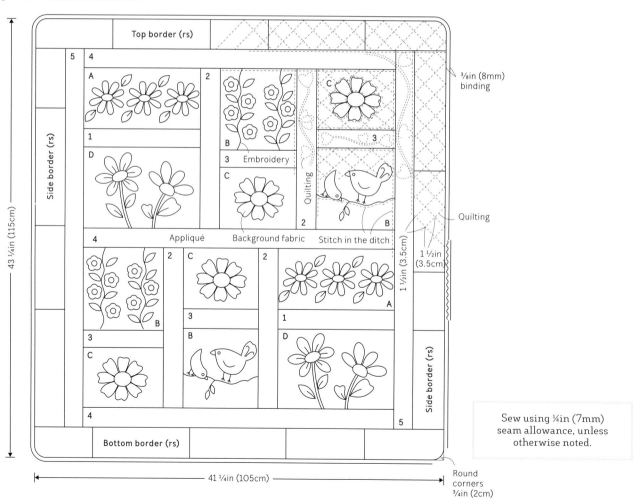

Cutting Instructions

Trace and cut out the templates on Pattern Sheet A. Cut out the following fabric pieces, adding ¼in (7mm) seam allowance:

Assorted scraps:
- Appliqué pieces

Cut out the following pieces, which do not have templates, according to the measurements below (these measurements include seam allowance):

Assorted scraps:
Background pieces
- A (cut 2): 6 ½ x 12 ¼in (16.4 x 31.4cm)
- B (cut 4): 8 ½in (21.4cm) square
- C (cut 4): 6 ½ x 8 ½in (16.4 x 21.4cm)
- D (cut 2): 8 ½ x 12 ¼in (21.4 x 31.4cm)

Border pieces
- 3 ½in (8.9cm) wide rectangles (cut a variety of lengths)

Sashing fabric:
- 1 (cut 2): 2 ½ x 12 ¼in (6.4 x 31.4cm)
- 2 (cut 4): 2 ½ x 16 ¼in (6.4 x 41.4cm)
- 3 (cut 4): 2 ½ x 8 ½in (6.4 x 21.4cm)
- 4 (cut 3): 2 ½ x 32in (6.4 x 81.4cm)
- 5 (cut 2): 2 ½ x 38in (6.4 x 96.4cm)

Binding fabric:
- Binding: 5yds (4.6m) of 1 ½in (3.5cm) wide single fold bias binding

Construction Steps

1. Appliqué the motifs to the background pieces as shown in the diagram on page 40. Refer to Figure 1 below for instructions on appliquéing the stems. Embroider as indicated on the templates (also refer to Figure 2 below for embroidery instructions).

2. Sew the sashing pieces to the blocks to create the quilt top, following the layout shown in the diagram on page 40.

3. Sew the border pieces together to create four borders measuring approximately 3 ½ x 42in (8.9 x 106.5cm). These will be trimmed down to fit the quilt top.

4. To add the side borders, measure the height of the pieced panel at both sides and the middle. Calculate the average height, then add ½in (1.4cm) for seam allowance. Trim the side borders to that measurement. Pin and sew the borders to the pieced panel.

5. To add the top and bottom borders, measure the width of the quilt (including the side borders) at the top, middle, and bottom. Calculate the average width, then add ½in (1.4cm) for seam allowance. Trim the top and bottom borders to that measurement. Pin and sew the borders to the quilt.

6. Make a mark ¾in (2cm) from each corner. Connect the adjacent marks with a curved line. Trim along the curves to create rounded corners.

7. Layer the top, batting, and backing. Quilt as shown in the diagram on page 40. Use the template on Pattern Sheet A to quilt the sashing.

8. Bind the quilt (refer to pages 33–34).

Figure 1: How to Appliqué the Stems

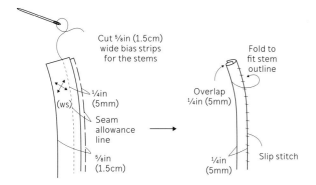

Figure 2: Embroidery Stitch Guide

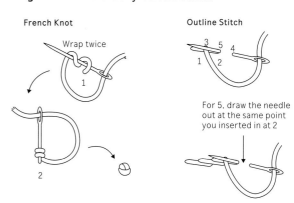

Patchwork Pencil Case

Shown on page 6

Materials

- **Patchwork fabric:** Assorted scraps

- **Main fabric:** One fat quarter of pink floral print fabric

- **Lining fabric:** One fat eighth of print fabric

- **Batting:** 8 x 8 ¾in (20 x 22cm)

- **Fusible fleece:** 2 ½ x 4 ¾in (6 x 12cm)

- ½yd (0.5m) of ⅜in (1cm) wide white lace

- One 7in (18cm) zipper

Layout Diagram

Diagram shows finished measurements

Body

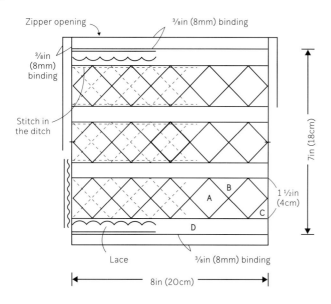

Zipper opening

⅜in (8mm) binding

⅜in (8mm) binding

Stitch in the ditch

7in (18cm)

1 ½in (4cm)

A B C D

Lace

⅜in (8mm) binding

8in (20cm)

Sides

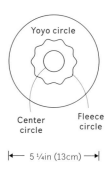

Yoyo circle

Center circle

Fleece circle

5 ¼in (13cm)

Sew using ¼in (7mm) seam allowance, unless otherwise noted.

Cutting Instructions

Trace and cut out the templates on Pattern Sheet A. Cut out the following fabric pieces, adding ¼in (7mm) seam allowance:

Assorted scraps:
- 15 A pieces
- 24 B pieces
- 12 C pieces

Main fabric:
- 4 D pieces
- 2 center circles
- 2 yoyo circles

Fusible fleece:
- 2 fleece circles

Cut out the following pieces, which do not have templates, according to the measurements below (these measurements include seam allowance):

Main fabric:
- Binding: 1yd (1m) of 1 ½in (3.5cm) wide single fold bias binding

Lining fabric:
- Lining: 7 ½ x 8 ½in (19.4 x 21.4cm)

Construction Steps

1. Sew pieces A–C together to create the three patchwork panels. Sew the patchwork panels and D pieces together to create the body. Layer the body, batting, and lining. Quilt as shown in the diagram. Bind the upper and lower edges.

2. Sew pieces of lace to the body, just below the bindings.

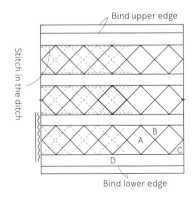

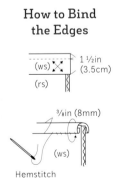

How to Bind the Edges

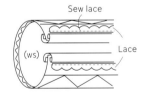

3. Sew the zipper to the binding on the inside of the case (refer to pages 36–37).

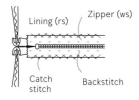

Lining (rs)
Zipper (ws)
Catch stitch
Backstitch

4. Bind the two ends of the case.

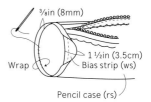

³⁄₈in (8mm)
1 ½in (3.5cm)
Bias strip (ws)
Wrap
Pencil case (rs)

5. Sew the center circle to the smooth side of the fleece circle. Next, adhere the fleece circle to the wrong side of the yoyo circle. Fold and press the edge of the yoyo circle over ³⁄₁₆in (5mm) to the wrong side. Running stitch, leaving long thread tails. Pull the thread tails to gather the circle into a yoyo. Secure the thread tails with a knot. Repeat to make another yoyo.

6. Working from the right side, hemstitch a yoyo to the binding on each end of the pencil case.

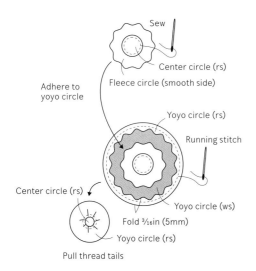

Sew
Center circle (rs)
Fleece circle (smooth side)
Adhere to yoyo circle
Yoyo circle (rs)
Running stitch
Center circle (rs)
Yoyo circle (ws)
Fold ³⁄₁₆in (5mm)
Yoyo circle (rs)
Pull thread tails

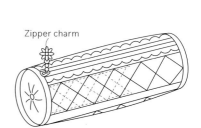

Hemstitch yoyo to binding
Yoyo (rs)
Pencil case (rs)

Zipper charm

Patchwork Scissor Caddy

Shown on page 6

Materials

- **Patchwork fabric:** Assorted scraps

- **Main fabric:** One fat eighth of light pink polka dot fabric

- **Lining fabric:** One fat eighth of print fabric

- **Binding fabric:** One fat eighth of pink floral print fabric

- **Batting:** 7 x 10 ¾in (18 x 27cm)

- One ⅜in (1cm) magnetic snap set

Layout Diagram

Diagram shows finished measurements

Sew using ¼in (7mm) seam allowance, unless otherwise noted.

Back

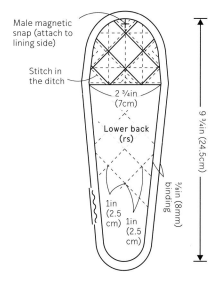

Male magnetic snap (attach to lining side)

Stitch in the ditch

2 ¾in (7cm)

Lower back (rs)

9 ¾in (24.5cm)

⅜in (8mm) binding

1in (2.5 cm) 1in (2.5 cm)

Front

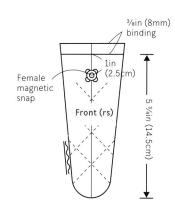

⅜in (8mm) binding

Female magnetic snap

1in (2.5cm)

Front (rs)

5 ¾in (14.5cm)

Cutting Instructions

Trace and cut out the templates on Pattern Sheet A. Cut out the following fabric pieces, adding ¼in (7mm) seam allowance:

Assorted scraps:
- Patchwork pieces

Main fabric:
- 1 lower back
- 1 front

Lining fabric:
- 1 back lining
- 1 front lining

Cut out the following pieces, which do not have templates, according to the measurements below (these measurements include seam allowance):

Binding fabric:
- Binding: ¾yd (0.7m) of 1 ½in (3.5cm) wide single fold bias binding

Construction Steps

1. Sew the patchwork pieces together, then use the template to trim into a flap shape, leaving ¼in (7mm) seam allowance around all edges. With right sides together, sew the flap to the lower back. Layer the assembled back, batting, and lining. Quilt as shown in the diagram.

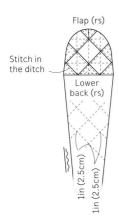

2. Layer the front, batting and lining. Quilt as shown in the diagram on page 45. Bind the upper edge of the front.

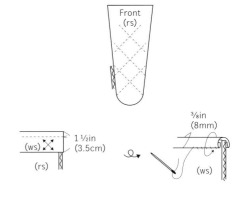

3. Align the front on top of the back lining and sew the pieces together. Bind the edges of the caddy. Attach the magnetic snap components following the placement indicated in the diagrams on page 45.

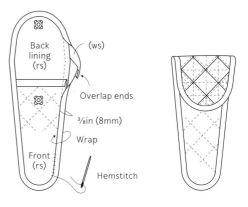

Dresden Plate Pin Cushion

Shown on page 7

Materials

- **Patchwork fabric:** Assorted scraps
- **Main fabric:** Two 4 ¾ x 5 ½in (12 x 14cm) pieces of pink floral print fabric
- **Lining fabric:** 4 ¾in (12cm) square of fabric
- **Batting:** 4 ¾in (12cm) square
- Polyester stuffing
- 19 ¾in (50cm) of ½in (1.2cm) wide lace

Layout Diagram

Diagram shows finished measurements

Front

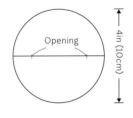

Back

Cutting Instructions

Trace and cut out the templates on Pattern Sheet A. Cut out the following fabric pieces, adding ¼in (7mm) seam allowance:

Assorted scraps:
- 8 petals
- 1 flower center

Main fabric:
- 1 front
- 2 backs

Lining fabric:
- 1 front

Sew using ¼in (7mm) seam allowance, unless otherwise noted.

Construction Steps

1. Sew the eight petals together, stopping at the seam allowance. Make the flower center as shown in the diagram, then appliqué to the petals. Appliqué the completed flower to the front.

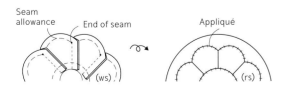

How to Make the Flower Center

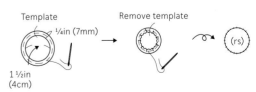

Running stitch seam allowance

Pull thread tails to gather, then remove template

Press with iron, then appliqué to flower

2. Layer the front, batting, and lining. Quilt as shown.

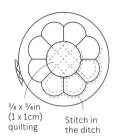

⅜ x ⅜in
(1 x 1cm)
quilting

Stitch in
the ditch

3. Align the two back pieces with right sides together. Sew along the straight edge, leaving a 2 ¾in (7cm) opening. Press the seam open.

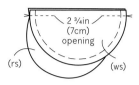

2 ¾in
(7cm)
opening

(rs)   (ws)

4. Align the front and back with right sides together. Sew around the circle.

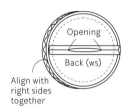

Opening

Back (ws)

Align with
right sides
together

5. Turn right side out through the opening. Stuff, then handstitch the opening closed.

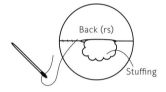

Back (rs)

Stuffing

6. Sew the two short ends of the lace with right sides together. Running stitch around the inner edge of the lace circle, then pull the thread tails to gather. Handstitch the lace to the pin cushion, covering the seam. The stitches should be visible on the back only.

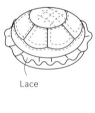

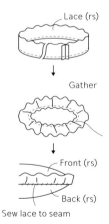

Lace (rs)

Gather

Lace

Front (rs)

Back (rs)

Sew lace to seam

Log Cabin Pin Cushion

Shown on page 7

Materials

- **Patchwork fabric:** Nine assorted scraps

- **Back fabric:** 4 x 4 ¾in (10 x 12cm)

- **Lining fabric:** 3 ½ x 4 ¾in (9 x 12cm)

- **Batting:** 3 ½ x 4 ¾in (9 x 12cm)

- Polyester stuffing

- 25 ½in (65cm) of ¾in (1.8cm) wide lace

Layout Diagram

Diagram shows finished measurements

Sew using ¼in (7mm) seam allowance, unless otherwise noted.

Front

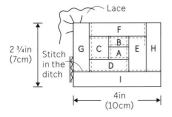

2 ¾in (7cm)

Stitch in the ditch

Lace

F
G C B E H
A
D
I

4in (10cm)

Back

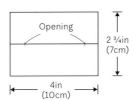

Opening

2 ¾in (7cm)

4in (10cm)

Cutting Instructions

Trace and cut out the templates on Pattern Sheet A. Cut out the following fabric pieces, adding ¼in (7mm) seam allowance:

Assorted scraps:
- 1 A piece
- 1 B piece
- 1 C piece
- 1 D piece
- 1 E piece
- 1 F piece
- 1 G piece

- 1 H piece
- 1 I piece

Cut out the following pieces, which do not have templates, according to the measurements below (these measurements include seam allowance):

Lining fabric:
- Lining: 3 ¼ x 4 ½in (8.4 x 11.4cm)

Back fabric:
- Backs (cut 2): 1 ⅞ x 4 ½in (4.9 x 11.4cm)

Construction Steps

1. To make the patchwork top, sew pieces A–I together in alphabetical order.

2. Layer the front, batting, and lining. Quilt as shown.

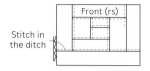

3. Align the two back pieces with right sides together. Sew along one long edge, leaving a 2 ¾in (7cm) opening. Press the seam open.

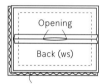

4. Align the front and back with right sides together. Sew around the edges.

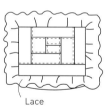

5. Turn right side out through the opening. Stuff, then handstitch the opening closed. Sew the two short ends of the lace with right sides together. Running stitch around the inner edge of the lace rectangle, then pull the thread tails to gather. Handstitch the lace to the pin cushion, covering the seam. The stitches should be visible on the back only.

Shoofly Pin Cushion

Shown on page 7

Materials

- **Patchwork fabric:** Five assorted scraps

- **Main fabric:** One yellow fat eighth

- **Lining fabric:** 4 ¾in (12cm) square

- **Batting:** 4 ¾in (12cm) square

- Polyester stuffing

- Eight ½in (1.2cm) pompoms

Layout Diagram

Diagram shows finished measurements

Sew using ¼in (7mm) seam allowance, unless otherwise noted.

Front

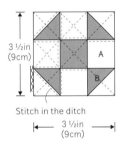

3 ½in (9cm)

A

B

Stitch in the ditch

3 ½in (9cm)

Back

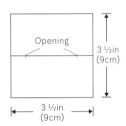

Opening

3 ½in (9cm)

3 ½in (9cm)

Cutting Instructions

Trace and cut out the templates on Pattern Sheet A. Cut out the following fabric pieces, adding ¼in (7mm) seam allowance:

Assorted scraps:
- 1 A piece
- 4 B pieces

Main fabric:
- 4 A pieces
- 4 B pieces

Cut out the following pieces, which do not have templates, according to the measurements below (these measurements include seam allowance):

Lining fabric:
- Lining: 4in (10.4cm) square

Main fabric:
- Backs (cut 2): 2 ¼ x 4in (5.9 x 10.4cm)

Construction Steps

1. With right sides together, align one main fabric B with one scrap fabric B. Sew together along the diagonal edge to form a square. Press the seam open. Repeat to make three more pieced squares. Next, sew the four pieced squares and the five A pieces together as shown. Press the seams open.

2. Layer the front, batting, and lining. Quilt as shown.

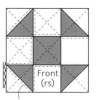

Front (rs)

Stitch in the ditch

3. Align the two back pieces with right sides together. Sew along one long edge, leaving a 2 ½in (6cm) opening. Press the seam open.

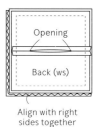

2 ½in (6cm) opening

Back (ws)

4. Align the front and back with right sides together. Sew around the edges.

Opening

Back (ws)

Align with right sides together

6. Turn right side out through the opening. Stuff, then handstitch the opening closed. Sew two pompoms to each corner.

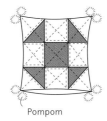

Pompom

Sewing Kit

Shown on page 8

Layout Diagram

Diagram shows finished measurements

Case Outside

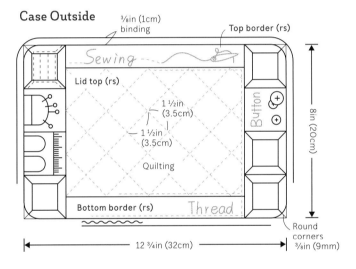

- ³⁄₈in (1cm) binding
- Top border (rs)
- Sewing
- Lid top (rs)
- 1 ½in (3.5cm)
- 1 ½in (3.5cm)
- Quilting
- Button
- 8in (20cm)
- Bottom border (rs)
- Thread
- 12 ¾in (32cm)
- Round corners ³⁄₈in (9mm)

Case Inside

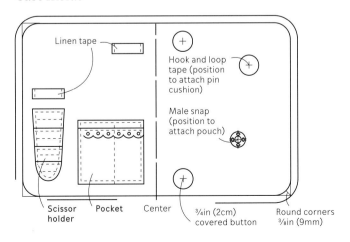

- Linen tape
- Hook and loop tape (position to attach pin cushion)
- Male snap (position to attach pouch)
- Scissor holder
- Pocket
- Center
- ¾in (2cm) covered button
- Round corners ³⁄₈in (9mm)

Sew using ¼in (7mm) seam allowance, unless otherwise noted.

Materials

(for all components of the kit)

- **Patchwork and appliqué fabric:** Assorted scraps

- **Backing fabric:** ⅓yd (0.3m) of fabric

- **Lining fabric:** ⅓yd (0.3m) of light pink floral fabric

- **Binding fabric:** ⅛yd (0.2m) of pink floral print fabric

- **Batting:** 8 ¾ x 13 ½in (22 x 34cm)

- **Fusible interfacing:** 3 ½ x 6in (9 x 15cm)

- **Fusible fleece:** 9 ¾ x 17 ¾in (25 x 45cm)

- No. 25 embroidery floss in dark brown, pink, and beige

- One ¾in (1.8cm) button

- Two ½in (1.3cm) buttons

- Four ¹⁄₁₆in (2mm) beads

- 5 ¼in (13cm) of ³⁄₈in (1cm) wide linen tape

- Two ¾in (2cm) covered buttons

- 16 ½in (42cm) of ⅛in (3mm) wide leather cord

- One ¾in (1.7cm) snap set

- One ¾in (2cm) circle of hook and loop tape

- 11in (28cm) of ³⁄₈in (8mm) wide lace

- One 20in (51cm) zipper

- One ½in (1.2cm) magnetic snap set

- One ¼ x ³⁄₈in (6 x 8mm) oval button

- 5in (2.5cm) square plastic sheet

- Polyester stuffing

Placement Guide

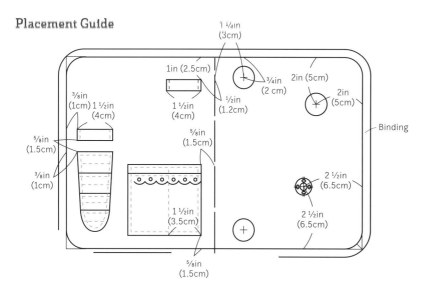

Cutting Instructions

Trace and cut out the templates on Pattern Sheet A. Cut out the following fabric pieces, adding ¼in (7mm) seam allowance:

Assorted scraps:
- 1 top border
- 1 bottom border
- 1 lid top
- Patchwork and appliqué pieces
- 2 pockets
- Scissor holder patchwork pieces

Backing fabric:
- 1 case
- 1 scissor holder

Lining fabric:
- 1 case

Batting:
- 1 case

Fusible fleece:
- 1 case

Fusible interfacing:
- 2 pockets
- 1 scissor holder

Cut out the following pieces, which do not have templates, according to the measurements below (these measurements include seam allowance):

Binding fabric:
- Zipper end bias strip: 1 ⅛ x 1 ¾in (2.9 x 4.4cm)
- Binding: 1 ¼yds (1.2m) of 1 ½in (3.5cm) wide single fold bias binding

Construction Steps

1. Make five spool blocks. These blocks are made with inset seams.

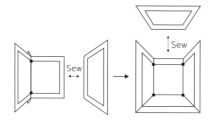

• = Start/stop sewing at seam allowance

2. Appliqué and embroider the top and bottom borders as indicated on the templates, then sew to the lid top. Appliqué and embroider the three remaining square blocks. Sew the appliquéd blocks and the spool blocks together in two columns of four, then sew to the lid top.

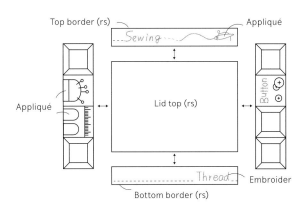

3. Layer the assembled top, batting, and backing. Quilt as shown. Trim the corners into a rounded shape as shown in the diagram on page 53.

4. Adhere fusible fleece to the wrong side of the case lining and trim the corners into a rounded shape. Attach two pieces of linen tape, two covered buttons, a piece of hook and loop tape and the male snap component to the right side of the lining following the placement noted in the diagram on page 54.

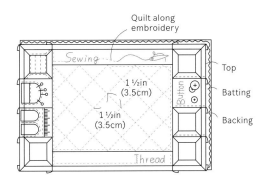

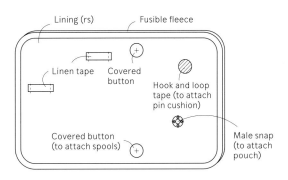

5. To make the pocket: Adhere fusible interfacing to the wrong side of both pocket pieces. Align with right sides together and sew, leaving a 1 ½in (4cm) opening. Turn right side out and topstitch along the upper edge. Topstitch a piece of lace to the pocket ¼in (5mm) from the upper edge. Sew the pocket to the lining following the placement noted in the diagram on page 54. Topstitch 1 ½in (3.5cm) from the right edge to divide the pocket into two sections. Make sure to sew a few reinforcing stitches at the top of the seam.

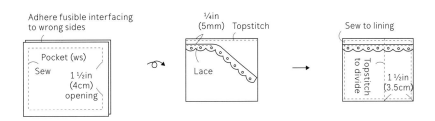

6. To make the scissor holder: Sew the patchwork pieces together to form the top. Adhere fusible interfacing to the wrong side. Sew the top and backing with right sides together, leaving a 1 ½in (4cm) opening. Turn right side out. Topstitch along the upper edge, then quilt with horizontal lines. Sew the scissor holder to the lining following the placement noted in the diagram on page 54.

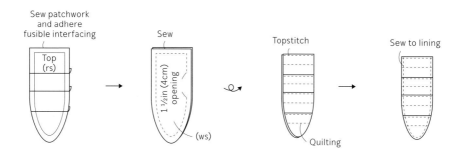

7. Align the case top and lining with wrong sides together. Baste the open zipper to the case. Use bias strips to bind the case and finish the zipper end as shown. Use the leather cord to make the spool holder as shown and attach to the covered buttons.

How to Make the Spool Holder

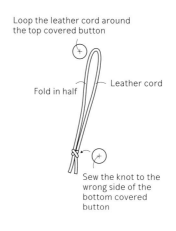

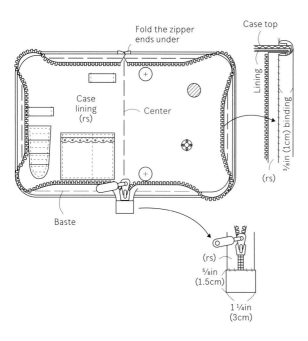

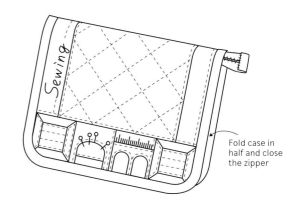

Pouch

Layout Diagram

Diagram shows finished measurements

Sew using ¼in (7mm) seam allowance, unless otherwise noted.

Flap

Inside: Male magnetic snap
Outside: Oval button

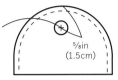

⅝in (1.5cm)

Inner Pocket

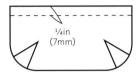

¼in (7mm)

Back

Female snap

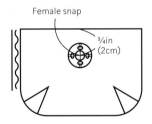

¾in (2cm)

Front

Female magnetic snap

1in (2.5cm)

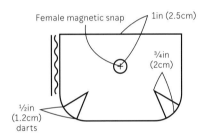

¾in (2cm)

½in (1.2cm) darts

Lining

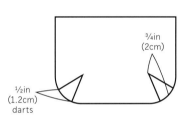

¾in (2cm)

½in (1.2cm) darts

Cutting Instructions

Trace and cut out the templates on Pattern Sheet A. Cut out the following fabric pieces, adding ¼in (7mm) seam allowance:

Assorted scraps:
- 2 pouches (create a patchwork pouch front if desired)
- 2 flaps

Backing fabric:
- 2 pouches

Lining fabric:
- 2 pouches
- 1 inner pocket

Fusible fleece:
- 2 pouches
- 1 flap

Cut out the following pieces, which do not have templates, according to the measurements below (these measurements include seam allowance):

Binding fabric:
- Binding: ⅓yd (0.3m) of ¾in (2cm) wide single fold bias binding

Construction Steps

1. Adhere fusible fleece to the wrong side of one of the pouch backings. Align one of the pouch pieces on top of the fleece, then quilt with vertical lines. Sew the darts. This will be the back.

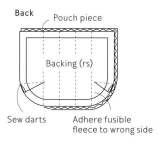

2. Adhere fusible fleece to the wrong side of the remaining pouch backing. Align the remaining pouch piece on top of the fleece. (**Note:** If creating a patchwork front, sew the pieces together to create the pouch piece.) Quilt with vertical lines, then embroider using two strands of floss. This will be the front. Sew the female magnetic snap to the front (refer to the template for placement). Sew the darts.

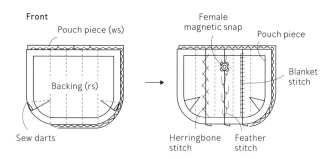

Embroidery Guide

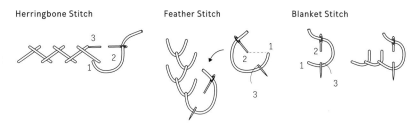

3. Sew the front and back with right sides together, leaving the pouch top open. Fold the darts in opposite directions on the front and back.

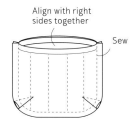

4. Sew the darts in the two pouch linings and the inner pocket. Fold the upper edge of the inner pocket over ¼in (7mm) and topstitch. Baste the inner pocket to the right side of one of the linings. This will be the back lining. Sew the front and back lining with right sides together, leaving the pouch top open.

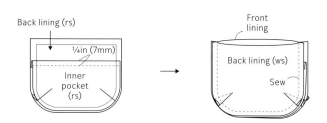

5. Adhere fusible fleece to the wrong side of one flap. Sew a scrap of fabric to the wrong side of the other flap to create a support for the magnetic snap (refer to the template for placement). Align the two flaps with right sides together and sew around the curve, leaving the bottom open. Turn right side out and topstitch the flap close to the edge. Handstitch a piece of lace to the right side of the flap along the curve.

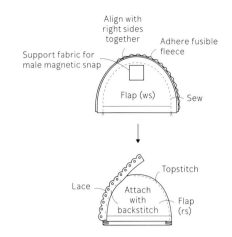

6. Sew the flap to the pouch back with right sides together. Bind the pouch opening using the bias strip.

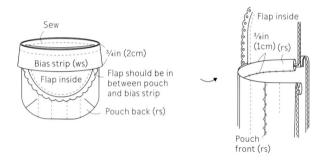

7. Sew the female snap to the pouch back following placement shown in the diagram on page 57. This will allow you to attach the pouch to the case lining. Sew the male magnetic snap to the flap inside. Sew the oval button to the flap outside.

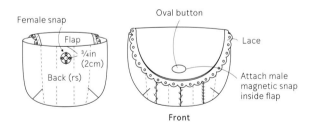

Pin Cushion

Layout Diagram

Diagram shows finished measurements

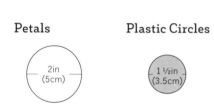

Top

2 ¾in
(7cm)

Bottom

2in
(5cm)

Petals

2in
(5cm)

Plastic Circles

1 ½in
(3.5cm)

Cutting Instructions

Trace and cut out the templates on Pattern Sheet A. Cut out the following pieces without adding seam allowance:

Assorted scraps:
- 1 top
- 1 bottom
- 10 petals

Plastic sheet:
- Two 1 ½in (3.5cm) circles

Do not add seam allowance when cutting out the pieces for this project.

Construction Steps

1. Running stitch around the top using ¼in (5mm) seam allowance. Leave long thread tails. Align a handful of stuffing and a plastic circle on the wrong side of the top. Pull the thread tails to gather the fabric around the plastic circle, then knot to secure. Use the same process to make the bottom, but do not use stuffing.

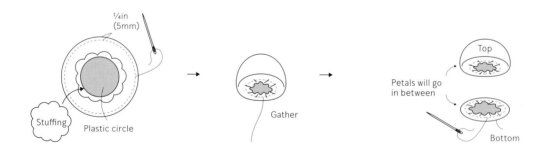

¼in
(5mm)

Stuffing

Plastic circle

Gather

Petals will go in between

Top

Bottom

2. Make 10 petals by folding and pressing as shown below.

3. Overlap the petals ⅜in (1cm). Running stitch using ¼in (5mm) seam allowance to sew the petals together. Leave long thread tails. Pull the thread tails to gather into a circle, then knot to secure the shape.

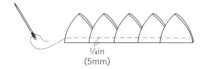

Sew 10 petals together in a circle using running stitch

4. Sew the petal circle to the top, then sew the bottom in place. Sew the remaining piece of hook and loop tape to the wrong side of the bottom. This will allow you to attach the pin cushion to the case lining.

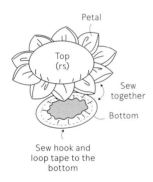

Yoyo Lanyards

Shown on page 10

Materials

- **Yoyo fabric:** Assorted scraps
- Five ¾in (2cm) lace flowers
- Assorted ¼in (4-6mm) sequins
- Assorted ⅟₁₆–⅛in (2-4mm) beads
- One ID card holder lanyard

Cutting Instructions

Trace and cut out the templates on Pattern Sheet A. Cut out a variety of small, medium, and large yoyos from the assorted scraps, without adding seam allowance.

Construction Steps

1. To make each yoyo, fold ⅛in (4mm) seam allowance to the wrong side. Running stitch the seam allowance, leaving long thread tails. Pull the thread tails taut to gather the yoyo into the desired finished size. Knot to secure.

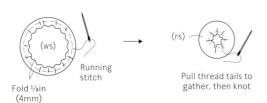

Fold ⅛in (4mm)

Running stitch

(ws)

(rs)

Pull thread tails to gather, then knot

Yoyo Finished Sizes	
Small	½in (1.3cm)
Medium	1in (2.5cm)
Large	1 ¼in (3cm)

2. Use the lace flowers, sequins, and beads to decorate the yoyos as desired.

Layer small yoyo and a bead on a large yoyo

Sequin and beads

Bead

Lace flower and bead

3. Arrange the yoyos in a chain equal in length to the lanyard. Join adjacent yoyos together with two whipstitches. Once all yoyos have been connected, sew to the lanyard.

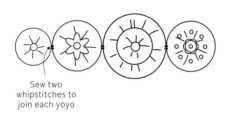

Sew two whipstitches to join each yoyo

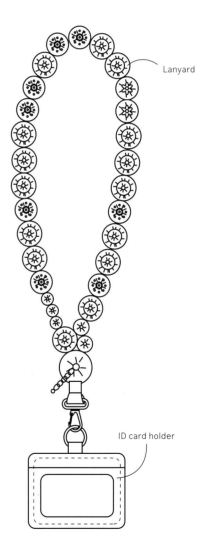

Lanyard

ID card holder

Floral Corsage Bracelet

Shown on page 10

Materials

- **Flower fabrics:** Eight 4in (10cm) squares of four assorted scrap fabrics (two squares of each fabric)

- **Support fabric:** 2in (5cm) square

- **Fusible web:** 8in (20cm) square

- One 4 ¾in (12cm) piece of ⅛in (3mm) wide leather cord in tan

- One 23 ¾in (60cm) piece of ⅛in (3mm) wide leather cord in each light green and dark green

- Three ¾in (2cm) wool felt balls

- Assorted ¹⁄₁₆in (2mm) beads

- Two ½in (1.2cm) shell buttons

- No. 8 pearl cotton in yellow green

Cutting Instructions

Trace and cut out the templates on Pattern Sheet A. Cut out the following fabric pieces, adding ¼in (7mm) seam allowance:

Support fabric:
- 1 support circle

Cut out the following pieces, which do not have templates, according to the measurements below:

Assorted scraps:
- Two 4in (10cm) squares of each fabric

Fusible web:
- Four 4in (10cm) squares

Construction Steps

1. To make the large flower: Adhere a square of fusible web to the wrong side of one fabric square. Adhere the other side of the fusible web square to the wrong side of the corresponding fabric square. Use the large flower template to trim the fabric into shape. Clip the opposite sides of the flower as indicated on the template. Follow the same process to make three small flowers.

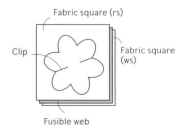

Fabric square (rs)

Clip

Fabric square (ws)

Fusible web

2. Layer the four flowers, right side up, with the large flower positioned on the bottom. Make sure that the clips in each flower line up. Use a piece of pearl cotton to tie the flowers together by inserting the pearl cotton through the clips. Tie a single knot in the pearl cotton and tighten it until the flowers are slightly puckered. Then secure the flowers with a second knot.

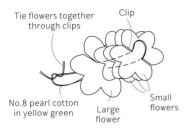

Tie flowers together through clips

Clip

No.8 pearl cotton in yellow green

Large flower

Small flowers

3. To make the support circle: Fold ⅛in (4mm) seam allowance to the wrong side. Running stitch the seam allowance, leaving long thread tails. Place the template on the wrong side of the fabric. Pull the thread tails to gather the fabric around the template. Press to secure the shape. Remove the template and hemstitch the circle to the wrong side of the large flower.

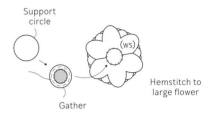

Support circle

(ws)

Gather

Hemstitch to large flower

4. Stitch the 4 ¾in (12cm) leather cord to the support circle. Next, stitch some beads to each wool felt ball. Set one ball aside. Stitch the other two balls together, and then use the leather cord to tie them to the bottom of the corsage.

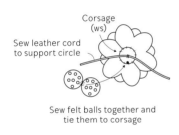

Corsage (ws)

Sew leather cord to support circle

Sew felt balls together and tie them to corsage

5. Fold both 23 ¾in (60cm) leather cords in half. Use pearl cotton to attach the remaining wool felt ball and one shell button to the bracelet following the placement indicated in the diagram.

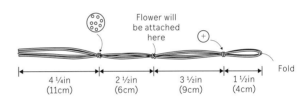

Attach wool felt ball and shell button with pearl cotton

Flower will be attached here

Fold

4 ¼in (11cm)

2 ½in (6cm)

3 ½in (9cm)

1 ½in (4cm)

6. Tie the flower to the bracelet using the leather cord from step 4 (refer to step 5 diagram for flower placement). Use pearl cotton to sew the remaining shell button to the flower center.

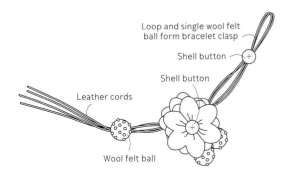

Loop and single wool felt ball form bracelet clasp

Shell button

Shell button

Leather cords

Wool felt ball

Lunch Tote

Shown on page 12

Materials

- **Patchwork fabric:** Assorted scraps

- **Main fabric:** ½yd (0.5m) of strawberry print fabric

- **Lining fabric:** ½yd (0.5m) of fabric

- **Batting:** 11 ¾ x 14 ¼in (30 x 36cm)

- One ⅝ x 1 ½in (1.5 x 4cm) piece of linen tape

- 55in (140cm) of ⅛in (3mm) diameter cord

- One set of 12in (20cm) handles

- No. 8 pearl cotton in pink

Layout Diagram

Diagram shows finished measurements

Sew using ¼in (7mm) seam allowance, unless otherwise noted.

Front, Bottom, and Back

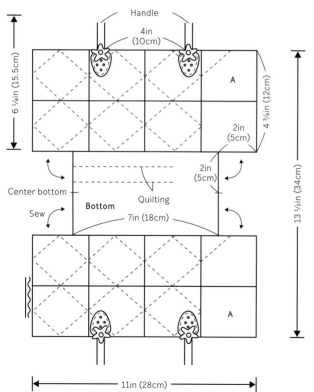

Drawstring Liner

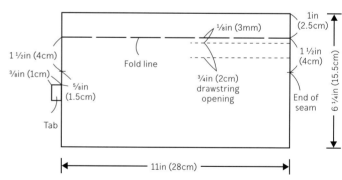

Cutting Instructions

Trace and cut out the templates on Pattern Sheet A. Cut out the following fabric pieces, adding ¼in (7mm) seam allowance:

Assorted scraps:
- 16 A pieces
- 4 cord charms

Cut out the following pieces, which do not have templates, according to the measurements below (these measurements include seam allowance):

Main fabric:
- Bottom: 4 ½ x 7 ½in (11.4 x 19.4cm)
- Drawstring liner (cut 2): 7 x 11 ¾in (17.5 x 30cm)
- Facing: 1 ½ x 22 ½in (4 x 57.4cm)

Lining fabric:
- Bias strips: ⅓yd (0.3m) of 1 ¼in (3cm) wide single fold bias strips

Construction Steps

1. Sew the A pieces together in rows of four, then sew two rows of four together to create the front. Repeat to create the back. With right sides together, sew one edge of the bottom to the front and the other edge to the back. Cut the lining out in the shape of the assembled top, adding ⅜in (8mm) extra seam allowance on the left and right edges. Layer the top, batting, and lining. Quilt as shown below.

2. Fold the bag in half with right sides together. Sew together along each side. On each side, trim the seam allowances, except for one lining layer. Wrap this seam allowance around the others and hemstitch to finish the seam.

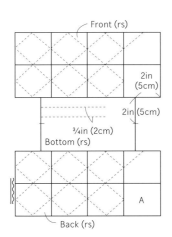

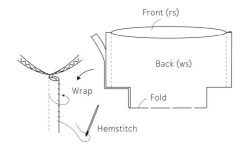

3. To miter each corner, align the side seam with the bottom fold. Mark a line across the corner where it measures 4in (10cm) wide. Stitch along the marked line. Use a bias strip to finish the seam allowance.

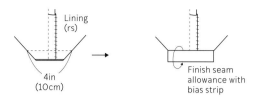

4. Align the two drawstring liners with right sides together with the folded tab sandwiched in between (refer to the diagram on page 66 for placement). Sew along the left and right edges, stopping at the end of seam marks.

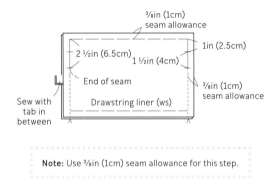

Note: Use ⅜in (1cm) seam allowance for this step.

5. Individually zigzag stitch the raw edges of the left and right sides. Press the seams open. Fold and press the drawstring opening seam allowances over and topstitch.

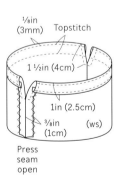

Topstitch drawstring opening on each side

6. To form the drawstring casing, fold and press the top edge over ⅜in (1cm), then another 1in (2.5cm). Topstitch ⅛in (3mm) from the top edge. Then topstitch another seam ⅛in (3mm) from the bottom fold.

7. Insert the drawstring liner into the bag with wrong sides together so that the side seams are aligned. (**Note:** The drawstring liner should be positioned so that the drawstring casing is facing down.) Baste in place. Make the facing: Sew the short ends with right sides together to create a loop. Next, align the facing and bag with right sides together. Sew all three layers together along the bag opening.

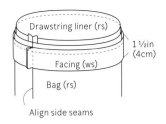

8. Backstitch the handles to the bag following placement indicated in the diagram on page 66. Take care to keep the facing and drawstring liner out of the way when attaching the handles.

9. Fold the facing to the inside of the bag. Fold the seam allowance under and hemstitch the facing to the drawstring liner.

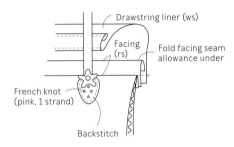

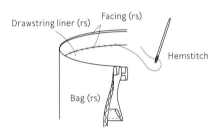

10. Cut the cord in half. Insert each piece through the drawstring casing. Make the cord charms as shown in the diagram.

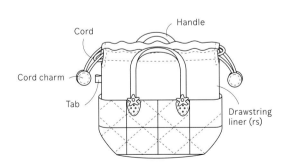

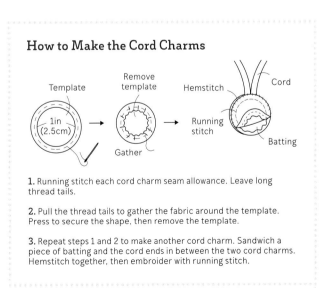

How to Make the Cord Charms

1. Running stitch each cord charm seam allowance. Leave long thread tails.

2. Pull the thread tails to gather the fabric around the template. Press to secure the shape, then remove the template.

3. Repeat steps 1 and 2 to make another cord charm. Sandwich a piece of batting and the cord ends in between the two cord charms. Hemstitch together, then embroider with running stitch.

Snack Satchel

Shown on page 12

Materials

- **Main fabric:** One fat quarter of strawberry print fabric

- **Bottom fabric:** One fat quarter of pink fabric

- ½yd (0.5m) of ⅜in (1cm) wide lace

- One ⅝ x 1 ½in (1.5 x 4cm) piece of linen tape

- 19 ¾in (50cm) of ⅛in (3mm) diameter cord

- One cord stopper

Layout Diagram

Diagram shows finished measurements

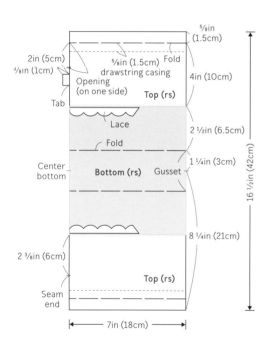

Sew using ¼in (7mm) seam allowance, unless otherwise noted.

Cutting Instructions

Cut out the following pieces according to the measurements below (these measurements include seam allowance):

Main fabric:
- Tops (cut 2): 5 x 7 ½in (12.7 x 19.4cm)

Bottom fabric:
- Bottom: 7 ½ x 8in (19.4 x 20.4cm)

Lace:
- Two 7 ½in (19.4cm) pieces

Construction Steps

1. Sew both top fabric pieces to the bottom fabric along the 7 ½in (19.4cm) edges. Sew the lace over both seams, positioning the top edge of the lace against the seam.

2. Fold the linen tape in half and pin to the top following the placement noted in the diagram on page 70. Fold the body in half with right sides together, then fold the bottom edge up 1 ¼in (3cm) to form the gusset. Sew the side seams, leaving the top 2 ⅜in (6cm) open on one side. This will be the drawstring opening. Finish the seams with zigzag stitch, then press them open.

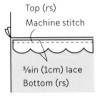

Top (rs)
Machine stitch
⅜in (1cm) lace
Bottom (rs)

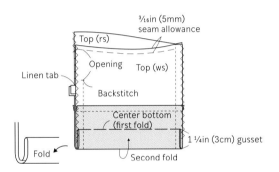

³⁄₁₆in (5mm) seam allowance
Top (rs)
Opening
Top (ws)
Linen tab
Backstitch
Center bottom (first fold)
1 ¼in (3cm) gusset
Fold
Second fold

3. Fold and press the drawstring opening seam allowances over and topstitch. Fold and press the top edge over ³⁄₁₆in (5mm), then another ⅝in (1.5cm). Topstitch to form the drawstring casing.

4. Turn the bag right side out. Press the bottom seams to make the folds crisp. Thread the cord through the casing. Thread the cord stopper onto the cord, and then knot the ends of the cord to secure the stopper in place.

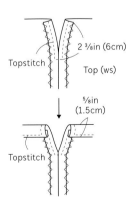

2 ⅜in (6cm)
Topstitch
Top (ws)
⅝in (1.5cm)
Topstitch

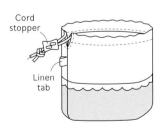

Cord stopper
Linen tab

71

Lunch Mat

Shown on page 12

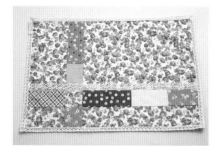

Materials

- **Main fabric:** One fat quarter of strawberry print fabric

- **Patchwork fabric:** Eight assorted scraps

- **Backing fabric:** One fat quarter

- **Inner lace:** ½yd (0.5m) of ¾in (2cm) wide lace

- **Border lace:** 1 ¾yds (1.5m) of ⅜in (1cm) wide lace

Layout Diagram

Diagram shows finished measurements

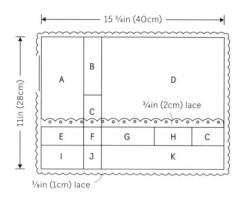

Sew using ¼in (7mm) seam allowance,
unless otherwise noted.

Cutting Instructions

Cut out the following pieces according to the measurements below (these measurements include seam allowance):

Main fabric:
- A: 4 x 8in (10.4 x 20.4cm)
- D: 8 x 11 ⅛in (20.4 x 28.4cm)
- I: 2 ½ x 4in (6.4 x 10.4cm)
- K: 2 ½ x 11 ⅛in (6.4 x 28.4cm)

Assorted scraps:
- B: 2 x 5 ¼in (5.4 x 13.4cm)
- C (cut 2): 2 x 3 ¼in (5.4 x 8.4cm)
- E: 2 x 4in (5.4 x 10.4cm)
- F: 2 x 2in (5.4 x 5.4cm)
- G: 2 x 5in (5.4 x 12.9cm)
- H: 2 x 3 ¾in (5.4 x 9.9cm)
- J: 2 x 2 ½in (5.4 x 6.4cm)

Backing fabric:
- Backing: 11 ½ x 16 ¼in (29.4 x 41.4cm)

Construction Steps

1. Sew pieces I–K together to make the bottom row. Sew pieces E–H and C together to make the middle row. Press the seams as indicated in the diagram. Sew the two rows together. Sew pieces A–D together to make the top section. Topstitch the inner lace to the lower edge of the top section, just above the seam allowance line. Then sew the top and bottom sections together. This will be the mat top.

2. Align the top and backing with right sides together. Sew along the edges, leaving a 4in (10cm) opening along the top edge. Turn the mat right side out and handstitch the opening closed. Press the edges.

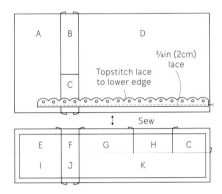

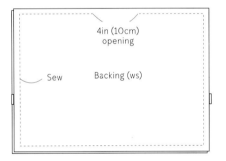

3. Topstitch around the edges of the mat. Then topstitch the border lace to the mat, folding the corners with a miter.

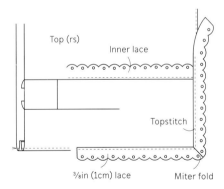

Patchwork Placemats

Shown on page 15

Materials

- **Patchwork fabric #1:** One fat quarter

- **Patchwork fabric #2:** One fat eighth

- **Patchwork fabric #3/ binding fabric:** One fat quarter

- **Backing fabric:** ⅓yd (0.3m)

- **Fusible fleece:** 9 ½ x 12 ¾in (24 x 32cm)

- One 3 ⅛in (8cm) circular Battenberg lace appliqué

- One 1 ½ x 6in (3.5 x 15cm) piece of Battenberg lace

- No. 8 pearl cotton in a coordinating or contrasting color

Layout Diagram

Diagram shows finished measurements

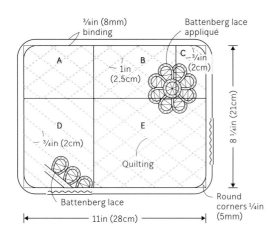

Sew using ¼in (7mm) seam allowance, unless otherwise noted.

Cutting Instructions

Cut out the following pieces according to the measurements below (these measurements include seam allowance):

Patchwork fabric #1:
- A: 3 ⅝ x 4 ⅝in (9.4 x 11.9cm)
- E: 5 ⅝ x 7 ⅜in (14.4 x 18.9cm)

Patchwork fabric #2:
- B: 3 ⅝ x 5 ⅝in (9.4 x 14.4cm)

Patchwork fabric #3/binding fabric:
- C: 2 ¼ x 3 ⅝in (5.9 x 9.4cm)
- D: 4 ⅝ x 5 ⅝in (11.9 x 14.4cm)
- Binding: 1 ¼yds (1.2m) of 1 ½in (3.5cm) wide single fold bias binding

Backing fabric:
- Backing: 8 ¾ x 11 ½in (22.4 x 29.4cm)

Construction Steps

1. Sew pieces A–E together to create the patchwork top.

2. Adhere fusible fleece to the wrong side of the patchwork top. Layer the backing underneath and quilt the three layers together.

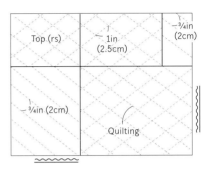

3. Make a mark ¼in (5mm) from each corner. Connect the adjacent marks with a curved line. Trim along the curves to create rounded corners.

4. Position the lace appliqués as desired. Use the pearl cotton to running stitch in place. Bind the edges of the placemat.

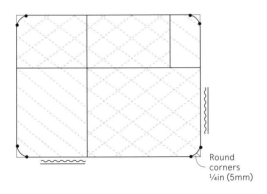

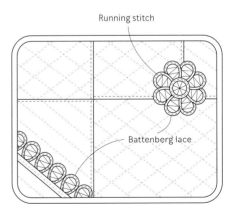

Heart Tea Pot Cozy

Shown on page 14

Materials

- **Heart fabrics:** 7in (18cm) scraps of six assorted prints

- **Heart backing fabric:** One fat quarter

- **Fabric A:** ½yd (0.5m) of beige polka dot fabric

- **Fabric B:** ⅝yd (0.6m) of beige checkered fabric

- **Lining fabric:** ⅓yd (0.3m)

- **Heavyweight fusible fleece:** 11 ¾ x 39 ½in (30 x 100cm)

- **Batting:** Small scrap

- **Loop fabric:** Small scrap

- No. 8 pearl cotton in red

Layout Diagram

Diagram shows finished measurements

Sew using ¼in (7mm) seam allowance, unless otherwise noted.

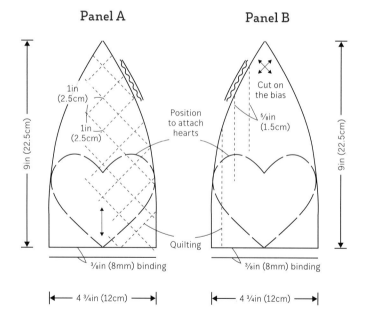

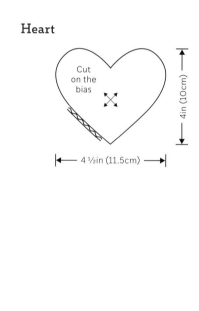

Cutting Instructions

Trace and cut out the templates on Pattern Sheet B. Cut out the following fabric pieces, adding ¼in (7mm) seam allowance:

Fabric A:
- 3 panels

Fabric B:
- 3 panels (cut on the bias)

Lining fabric:
- 6 panels

Heart fabric:
- 6 outside hearts (cut on the bias)

Heart backing fabric:
- 6 heart tops
- 6 heart bottoms

Fusible fleece:
- 12 panels
- 6 hearts (do not add seam allowance)

Cut out the following pieces, which do not have templates, according to the measurements below (these measurements include seam allowance):

Fabric B:
- Binding: 1yd (1m) of 1 ½in (3.5cm) wide single fold bias binding

Loop fabric:
- Loops (cut 2 on the bias): 1 ½ x 4 ¾in (3.5 x 12cm)

Batting:
- Batting strips (cut 2): 2 ½ x 4in (6 x 10cm)

Construction Steps

1. Adhere fusible fleece to the wrong side of each A and B panel, then quilt as shown in the diagrams on page 76. With right sides together, sew the A and B panels together alternately to create the tea cozy. Press the seam allowances open and hemstitch to the fusible fleece on the inside.

2. Follow the same process used in step 1 to make the lining. Insert the lining into the tea cozy with wrong sides together. Use the bias strips to bind the bottom edge.

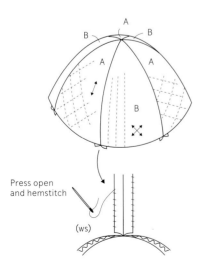

Press open and hemstitch

(ws)

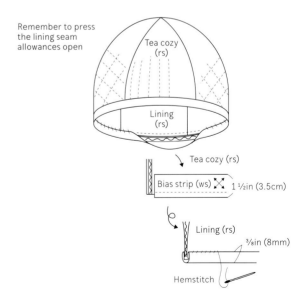

Remember to press the lining seam allowances open

Tea cozy (rs)

Lining (rs)

Tea cozy (rs)

Bias strip (ws) 1 ½in (3.5cm)

Lining (rs)

⅜in (8mm)

Hemstitch

3. To make the heart backing, sew a heart top to a heart bottom, leaving a 2in (5cm) opening. Press the seam open. Adhere fusible fleece to the wrong side of an outside heart. With right sides together, sew the outside heart to the pieced heart backing. Make a clip in the V section of the seam allowance. Turn right side out and hemstitch the opening closed on the backing. Embroider the heart with French knots. Repeat to make a total of six hearts.

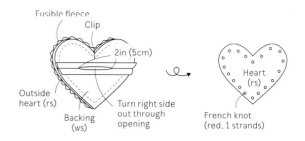

Fusible fleece
Clip
2in (5cm)
Outside heart (rs)
Turn right side out through opening
Backing (ws)
Heart (rs)
French knot (red, 1 strands)

4. Sew the hearts to the tea cozy following the placement indicated on the template. Make the loops as shown in the diagram and sew to the top.

Loop
Sew loops to the tea cozy
Sew hearts to the tea cozy

How to Make the Loops

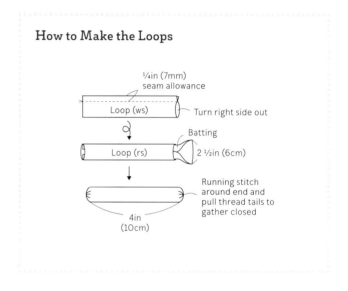

¼in (7mm) seam allowance
Loop (ws)
Turn right side out
Loop (rs)
Batting
2 ½in (6cm)
Running stitch around end and pull thread tails to gather closed
4in (10cm)

Heart Tea Pot Mat

Shown on page 14

Materials

- **Heart fabric:** 4in (10cm) scraps of eight assorted prints
- **Heart backing fabric:** One fat eighth
- **Circle fabric:** One fat eighth
- **Heavyweight fusible fleece:** 9 ¾ x 14 ¼in (25 x 36cm)
- No. 8 pearl cotton in red

Layout Diagram

Diagram shows finished measurements

Sew using ¼in (7mm) seam allowance, unless otherwise noted.

Heart

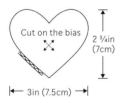

Cut on the bias

2 ¾in (7cm)

3in (7.5cm)

Circle

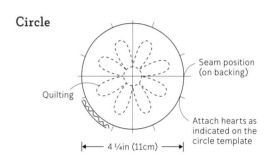

Seam position (on backing)

Quilting

Attach hearts as indicated on the circle template

4 ¼in (11cm)

Cutting Instructions

Trace and cut out the templates on Pattern Sheet B. Cut out the following fabric pieces, adding ¼in (7mm) seam allowance:

Heart fabric:
- 8 heart tops
- 8 heart bottoms
- 8 outside hearts (cut on the bias)

Circle fabric:
- 2 backing pieces
- 1 top

Fusible fleece (do not add seam allowance):
- 8 hearts
- 1 circle

Construction Steps

1. With right sides together, sew both circle backing pieces together, leaving a 1 ¾in (4.5cm) opening. Press the seam open. Adhere fusible fleece to the wrong side of the circle top. Sew the circle top and backing with right sides together. Turn right side out and hemstitch the opening closed on the backing. Quilt as indicated on the template.

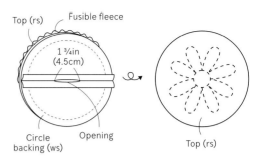

2. To make the heart backing, sew a heart top to a heart bottom, leaving a 1 ½in (3.5cm) opening. Press the seam open. Adhere fusible fleece to the wrong side of an outside heart. With right sides together, sew the outside heart to the pieced heart backing. Make a clip in the V section of the seam allowance. Turn right side out and hemstitch the opening closed on the backing. Embroider the heart with French knots. Repeat to make a total of eight hearts.

3. Use a few tack stitches to hand sew the hearts to the circle following the placement indicated on the circle template. Then hand sew adjacent hearts to each other using a few tack stitches. When sewing, make stitches through the hearts so they aren't visible from the right side of the mat.

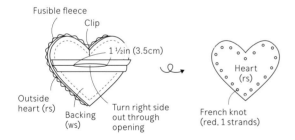

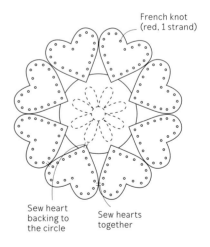

Strawberry Spring Mini Quilt

Shown on page 16

Materials

- **Patchwork and appliqué fabric:** Assorted scraps
- **Background fabric:** One fat eighth of polka dot fabric
- **Backing fabric:** One fat quarter
- **Binding fabric:** ¼yd (0.2m) of plaid fabric

- **Batting:** 11 x 13 ¾in (28 x 35cm)
- Three ¾in (2cm) lace flowers
- Three ¼in (6mm) sequins
- Three ¹⁄₁₆in (2mm) beads
- No. 25 embroidery floss in green and yellow green

Layout Diagram

Diagram shows finished measurements

Sew using ¼in (7mm) seam allowance, unless otherwise noted.

Refer to the Technique Guide on pages 29-34 for photos related to this project.

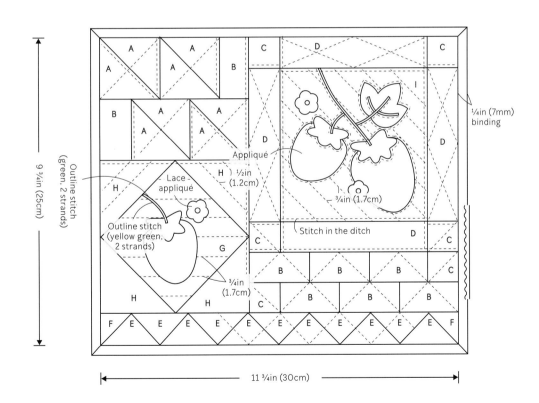

Cutting Instructions

Trace and cut out the templates on Pattern Sheet B. Cut out the following fabric pieces, adding ¼in (7mm) seam allowance:

Assorted scraps:
- Appliqué pieces
- 8 A pieces (4 dark, 4 light)
- 8 B pieces
- 6 C pieces
- 4 D pieces
- 11 E pieces (5 light, 6 dark)
- 2 F pieces (light)
- 4 H pieces (dark)

Background fabric:
- 1 G piece
- 1 I piece

Cut out the following pieces, which do not have templates, according to the measurements below (these measurements include seam allowance):

Backing fabric:
- Backing: 12 ¼ x 14 ¼in (31 x 36cm)

Binding fabric:
- Binding: 1 ⅓yds (1.2m) of 1 ½in (3.5cm) wide single fold bias binding

Construction Steps

1. Appliqué and embroider the motifs to the pieces of background fabric as shown in the diagram on page 81 (refer to the templates for embroidery instructions). (**Note:** Each stem is embroidered with two rows of outline stitch. Use two strands of yellow green for the left row and two strands of green for the right row).

2. Sew the patchwork pieces and the appliqué blocks together to create the quilt top, following the layout shown in the diagram on page 81.

3. Layer the top, batting, and backing. Quilt as shown in the diagram on page 81.

4. Bind the quilt (refer to pages 33–34).

5. Attach the lace flower appliqués as shown in Figure 1.

Figure 1: How to Attach a Lace Flower Appliqué

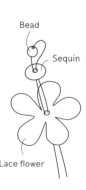

Bead

Sequin

Lace flower

Sweet Summertime Mini Quilt

Shown on page 17

Materials

- **Patchwork and appliqué fabric:** Assorted scraps

- **Background fabric #1:** One fat eighth of cherry print fabric

- **Background fabric #2:** One fat eighth of polka dot fabric

- **Border/binding fabric:** ½yd (0.5m) of pink print fabric

- **Backing fabric:** One fat quarter

- **Batting:** 13 ¾in (35cm) square

- No. 8 pearl cotton in pink and variegated green

Layout Diagram

Diagram shows finished measurements

Sew using ¼in (7mm) seam allowance, unless otherwise noted.

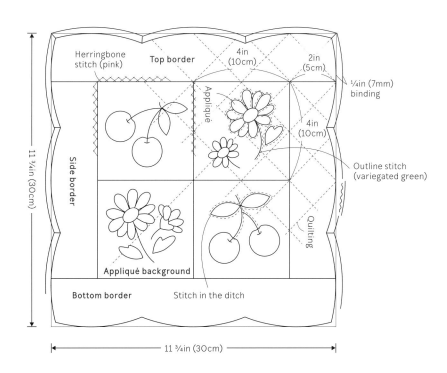

Cutting Instructions

Trace and cut out the templates on Pattern Sheet B. Cut out the following fabric pieces, adding ¼in (7mm) seam allowance:

Assorted scraps:
- Appliqué pieces

Cut out the following pieces, which do not have templates, according to the measurements below (these measurements include seam allowance):

Background fabric #1:
- Appliqué backgrounds (cut 2): 4 ½in (11.4cm) squares

Background fabric #2:
- Appliqué backgrounds (cut 2): 4 ½in (11.4cm) squares

Border/binding fabric:
- Side borders (cut 2): 2 ½ x 8 ½in (6.4 x 21.4cm)
- Top/bottom borders (cut 2): 2 ½ x 12 ¼in (6.4 x 31.4cm)
- Binding: 1 ½yds (1.4m) of 1 ½in (3.5cm) wide single fold bias binding

Backing fabric:
- Backing: 14in (36cm) square

Construction Steps

1. Appliqué and embroider the motifs to the pieces of background fabric as shown in the diagram on page 83 (refer to the templates for embroidery instructions). (**Note:** All stems are embroidered with two strands of No. 8 pearl cotton in variegated green).

2. Sew the appliqué blocks together and then add the border to create the quilt top, following the layout shown in the diagram on page 83.

3. Layer the top, batting, and backing. Quilt as shown in the diagram on page 83.

4. Use the template on Pattern Sheet B to mark and cut the border scallops and corners. Make sure to align the corner of the template with the corner of the quilt. The first scallop should end at the halfway point of the appliqué block.

5. Bind the quilt (refer to pages 33–34).

6. Embroider the seams around the blocks with herringbone stitch using No. 8 pearl cotton in pink.

Herringbone Stitch

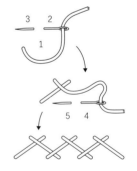

Autumn Symphony Wall Hanging

Shown on page 18

Materials

- **Patchwork and appliqué fabric:** Assorted scraps
- **Scallop fabric:** Assorted scraps of three coordinating prints
- **Backing/facing fabric:** ½yd (0.5m) of fabric
- **Batting:** 12 ¾ x 13 ½in (32 x 34cm)
- No. 25 embroidery floss in yellow and brown
- No. 8 pearl cotton in variegated yellow

Layout Diagram

Diagram shows finished measurements

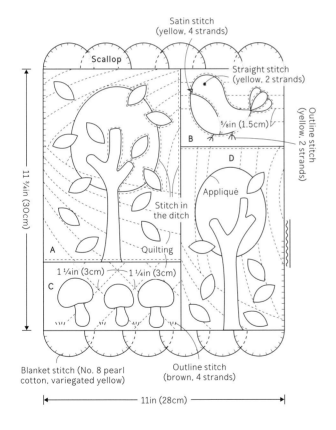

Satin stitch (yellow, 4 strands)

Scallop

Straight stitch (yellow, 2 strands)

⅝in (1.5cm)

Outline stitch (yellow, 2 strands)

B

D

Appliqué

Stitch in the ditch

11 ¾in (30cm)

1 ¼in (3cm) | 1 ¼in (3cm)

A

Quilting

C

Blanket stitch (No. 8 pearl cotton, variegated yellow)

Outline stitch (brown, 4 strands)

11in (28cm)

Sew using ¼in (7mm) seam allowance, unless otherwise noted.

Cutting Instructions

Trace and cut out the templates on Pattern Sheet B. Cut out the following fabric pieces, adding ¼in (7mm) seam allowance:

Assorted scraps:
- Appliqué pieces:
- 1 A piece
- 1 B piece
- 1 C piece
- 1 D piece

Scallop fabrics:
- 12 scallop fronts and 12 scallop backs (cut in matching fabric pairs)

Batting:
- 12 scallops

Cut out the following pieces, which do not have templates, according to the measurements below (these measurements include seam allowance):

Backing/facing fabric:
- Backing: 11 ½ x 12 ¼ in (29.4 x 31.4cm)
- Vertical facings (cut 2 on the bias): 1 ¼ x 12 ¼in (3.4 x 31.4cm)
- Horizontal facings (cut 2 on the bias): 1 ¼ x 11 ½in (3.4 x 29.4cm)

Construction Steps

1. Appliqué and embroider the motifs to the pieces of background fabric (A–D) as shown in the diagram on page 85 (refer to the templates for embroidery instructions).

2. Sew the appliqué blocks together following the layout shown in the diagram on page 85.

3. Layer the top, batting, and backing. Quilt as shown in the diagram on page 85.

4. With right sides together, sew a vertical facing to each long edge of the quilt. Fold the facing strip to the back and hemstitch in place. The finished facing will measure ¾in (2cm) wide.

5. Make the scallops (refer to Figure 1): Align two scallops with right sides together with a scallop of batting underneath. Sew together along the curve, leaving the straight edge open. Trim and clip the seam allowance, then turn right side out. Blanket stitch around the curve. Make 12 scallops.

6. With right sides together, align the straight edge of six scallops with the top edge of the quilt. The scallops should overlap evenly to match the width of the quilt. Baste in place. Repeat for the bottom edge of the quilt.

7. With right sides together, sew a horizontal facing to the top edge of the quilt, making sure the scallops are facing down. Fold the facing to the back. Fold the short raw edges in and hemstitch the facing in place. Repeat for the bottom edge of the quilt. Press the top and bottom edges so the scallops point away from the quilt (refer to Figure 2).

Figure 1: How to Make the Scallops

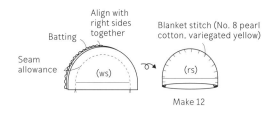

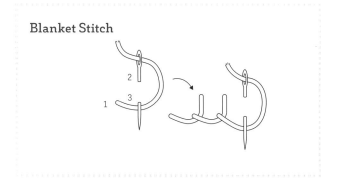

Blanket Stitch

Figure 2: How to Attach the Horizontal Facings

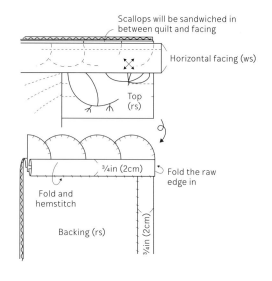

Winter Wonderland Wall Hanging

Shown on page 19

Materials

- **Appliqué fabric:** Assorted scraps

- **Background fabric:** One fat quarter of blue polka dot fabric

- **Accent fabric:** Scraps of green fabric

- **Backing fabric:** One fat quarter

- **Binding fabric:** One fat quarter of blue plaid fabric

- **Batting:** 12 ¾ x 13 ¾in (32 x 35cm)

- No. 25 embroidery floss in black and brown

- No. 5 pearl cotton in white

Layout Diagram

Diagram shows finished measurements

Sew using ¼in (7mm) seam allowance, unless otherwise noted.

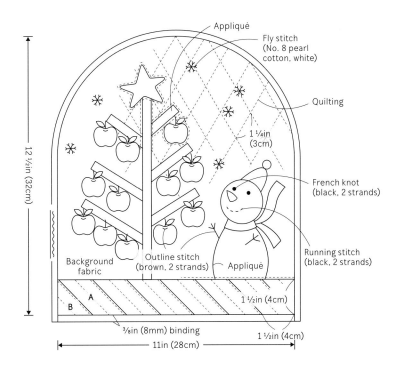

Cutting Instructions

Trace and cut out the templates on Pattern Sheet B. Cut out the following fabric pieces, adding ¼in (7mm) seam allowance:

Assorted scraps:
- Appliqué pieces:

Background fabric:
- 1 background
- 3 A pieces
- 1 B piece

Accent fabric:
- 3 A pieces
- 1 B piece

Cut out the following pieces, which do not have templates, according to the measurements below (these measurements include seam allowance):

Backing fabric:
- Backing: 13in (33cm) square

Binding fabric:
- Short binding: One 1 ½ x 12 ¾in (3.5 x 32cm) single fold bias strip
- Long binding: One 1 ½ x 39 ½in (3.5 x 100cm) single fold bias strip

Construction Steps

1. Appliqué and embroider the motifs to the background fabric as shown in the diagram on page 87 (refer to the templates for embroidery instructions).

2. Sew the A and B pieces together following the layout shown in the diagram on page 87. Then sew the pieced border to the bottom edge of the appliquéd panel.

3. Layer the top, batting, and backing. Quilt as shown in the diagram on page 87. Trim the batting and backing to match the quilt top.

4. Use the shorter binding to bind the bottom edge of the quilt and the long binding to bind the curved edge of the quilt (refer to pages 33–34).

Fly Stitch

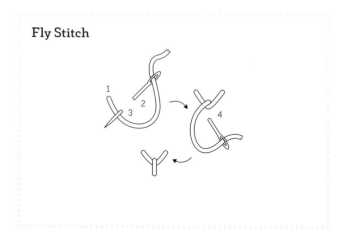

Floral Appliqué Tote

Shown on page 20

Materials

- **Appliqué fabric:** Assorted scraps
- **Main fabric:** ⅝yd (0.6m) of polka dot fabric
- **Gusset fabric:** ¼yd (0.25m) of plaid fabric
- **Lining/piping fabric:** 1yd (1m) of floral print fabric
- **Backing fabric:** ⅝yd (0.6m)
- **Fusible fleece:** 18 ¼ x 22 ½in (46 x 57cm)
- 1 ½yds (1.2m) of ¹⁄₁₆in (2mm) diameter cord
- 7in (18cm) of ⅜in (8mm) wide lace
- 3 ½in of ⅛in (3mm) diameter leather cord
- One ¾in (1.8cm) covered button

Layout Diagram

Diagram shows finished measurements

Sew using ¼in (7mm) seam allowance, unless otherwise noted.

Front/Back Body

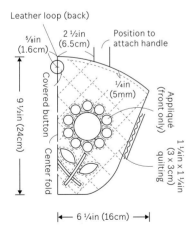

- Leather loop (back)
- ⅝in (1.6cm)
- 2 ½in (6.5cm)
- Position to attach handle
- Covered button
- ¼in (5mm)
- Appliqué (front only)
- Center fold
- 1 ¼in x 1 ¼in (3 x 3cm) quilting
- 9 ½in (24cm)
- 6 ¼in (16cm)

Front/Back Lining

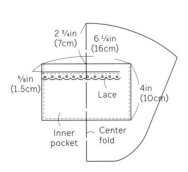

- 2 ¾in (7cm)
- 6 ¼in (16cm)
- ⅝in (1.5cm)
- Lace
- 4in (10cm)
- Inner pocket
- Center fold

Gusset

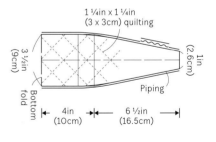

- 1 ¼in x 1 ¼in (3 x 3cm) quilting
- 3 ½in (9cm)
- 1in (2.6cm)
- Bottom fold
- Piping
- 4in (10cm)
- 6 ½in (16.5cm)

Gusset Lining

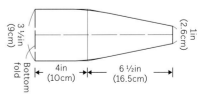

- 3 ½in (9cm)
- 1in (2.6cm)
- Bottom fold
- 4in (10cm)
- 6 ½in (16.5cm)

Handle

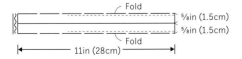

- Fold
- ⅝in (1.5cm)
- ⅝in (1.5cm)
- Fold
- 11in (28cm)

Cutting Instructions

Trace and cut out the templates on Pattern Sheet C. Cut out the following fabric pieces, adding ¼in (7mm) seam allowance:

Assorted scraps:
*   Appliqué pieces (cut on the bias if noted on template)

Cut out the following fabric pieces, adding ⅜in (1cm) seam allowance:

Main fabric:
*   2 bag bodies

Gusset fabric:
*   1 gusset

Backing fabric:
*   2 bag bodies
*   1 gusset

Lining fabric:
*   2 bag bodies
*   1 gusset

Fusible fleece:
*   2 bag bodies
*   1 gusset

Cut out the following pieces, which do not have templates, according to the measurements below (these measurements include seam allowance):

Lining/piping fabric:
*   Piping bias strips: Two 1 ¼ x 23 ¾in (3 x 58cm) single fold bias strips

Main fabric:
*   Inner pocket: 5 ⅛ x 6 ¾in (12.9 x 17.4cm)
*   Handles (cut 2): 1 ¾ x 11 ½in (4.4 x 29.4cm)

Gusset fabric:
*   Handles (cut 2): 1 ¾ x 11 ½in (4.4 x 29.4cm)

Fusible fleece:
*   Handles (cut 4): 1 ¼ x 11 ½in (3 x 29.4cm)

Construction Steps

1. Appliqué the floral motif to the front body (refer to the template for placement).

2. Adhere fusible fleece to the wrong side of the front body, then layer on top of the backing. Quilt as shown.

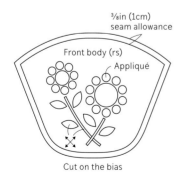

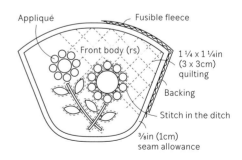

3. Adhere fusible fleece to the wrong side of the back body, then layer on top of the backing. Quilt as shown. Follow the same process to make the gusset.

4. To make the piping, fold each piping bias strip around a piece of cord with right sides facing out. Baste, stitching ⅛in (3mm) from the fold.

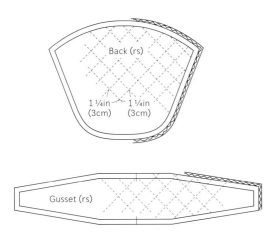

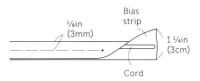

5. Baste the piping to the front and back bodies. With right sides together, sew the gusset to the front and back bodies.

6. With right sides together, sew the gusset lining to the body linings, leaving a 4in (10cm) opening at the bottom. To make the inner pocket, fold and press the seam allowances under. Fold and press the upper edge of the pocket over ⅝in (1.5cm). Topstitch the lace to the pocket ⅝in (1.5cm) from the upper edge. Topstitch the pocket to the lining following placement noted in the diagram on page 89.

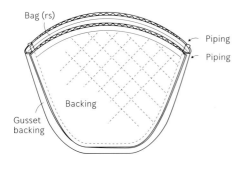

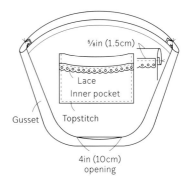

7. To make the handles: Adhere fusible fleece to the wrong side of each handle piece. With right sides together, align one handle cut from main fabric with another handle cut from gusset fabric. Sew together along the long edges. Press the seam allowances open. Turn right side out. Align the seam along the center of the handle. Topstitch each long edge, stitching as close to the edge as possible. Repeat to make another handle.

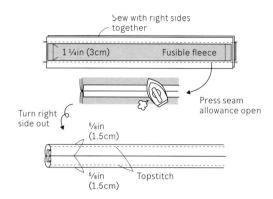

Sew with right sides together

1 ¼in (3cm)   Fusible fleece

Press seam allowance open

Turn right side out

⅝in (1.5cm)

⅝in (1.5cm)   Topstitch

8. Baste the handles and leather loop to the bag (refer to the diagram on page 89 for placement). Insert the bag into the lining with right sides together. Sew together along the bag opening.

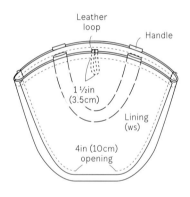

Leather loop

Handle

1 ½in (3.5cm)

Lining (ws)

4in (10cm) opening

9. Turn the bag right side out through the opening in the lining. Tuck the lining inside the bag and hemstitch closed. Topstitch the bag opening. Sew the covered button to the bag front (refer to the diagram on page 89 for placement).

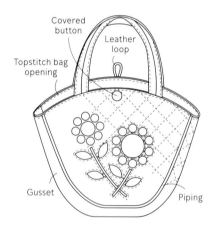

Covered button

Leather loop

Topstitch bag opening

Gusset

Piping

Scallop Pouch

Shown on page 20

Sew using ¼in (7mm) seam allowance, unless otherwise noted.
Refer to the Technique Guide on pages 35-37 for photos related to this project.

Materials

- **Patchwork fabric:** Assorted scraps
- **Main fabric:** One fat quarter of plaid fabric
- **Lining fabric:** ¼yd (0.25m) of fabric
- **Batting:** 8 x 12 ¼in (20 x 31cm)
- One 8in (20cm) zipper
- No. 8 pearl cotton in variegated green

Layout Diagram

Diagram shows finished measurements

Front

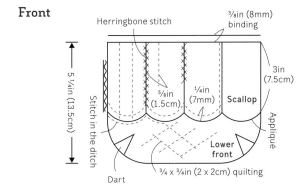

Herringbone stitch
⅜in (8mm) binding
3in (7.5cm)
⅝in (1.5cm)
¼in (7mm)
Scallop
Appliqué
Stitch in the ditch
Lower front
5 ¼in (13.5cm)
Dart
¾ x ¾in (2 x 2cm) quilting
7in (18cm)

Back

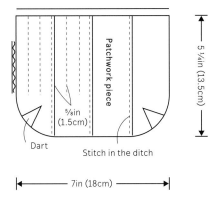

Patchwork piece
⅝in (1.5cm)
5 ¼in (13.5cm)
Dart
Stitch in the ditch
7in (18cm)

Cutting Instructions

Trace and cut out the templates on Pattern Sheet C. Cut out the following fabric pieces, adding ¼in (7mm) seam allowance:

Assorted scraps:
- 4 scallops (for front)
- 4 patchwork pieces (for back)

Main fabric:
- 1 lower front

Cut out the following fabric pieces, adding ⅝in (1.5cm) seam allowance:

Lining fabric:
- 1 front
- 1 back

Cut out the following piece, which does not have a template, according to the measurements below (these measurements include seam allowance):

Main fabric:
- Binding: One 1 ½ x 15in (3.5 x 38cm) single fold bias strip

Construction Steps

1. Sew the four scallops together, stopping at the end of seam marks. Appliqué to the pouch lower front (refer to the template for placement). Layer the front, batting, and lining. Embroider and quilt as shown. Sew the darts.

2. Sew the patchwork pieces together to create the back. Layer the back, batting, and lining. Quilt as shown. Sew the darts.

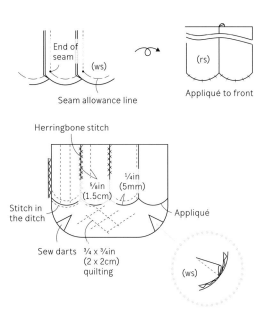

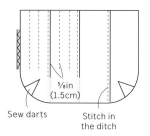

3. Using ⅝in (1.5cm) seam allowance, sew the front and back with right sides together, leaving the pouch top open. Trim the seam allowances, except for one lining layer. Wrap this seam allowance around the others and hemstitch to finish the seam.

4. Bind the pouch opening using the bias strip. Sew the zipper to the inside of the pouch as shown.

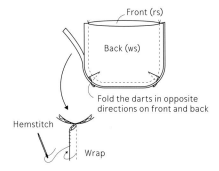

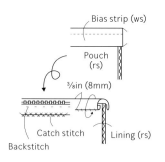

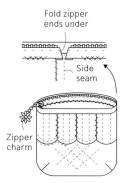

Hexagon Zip Pouch

Shown on page 21

Materials

- **Patchwork fabric:** Assorted scraps
- **Main fabric:** ½yd (0.5m) of strawberry print fabric
- **Lining fabric:** ½yd (0.5m)
- **Batting:** 11 ¾ x 13 ¾in (30 x 35cm)
- **One 8in (20cm) zipper**

Sew using ⅝in (1.5cm) seam allowance, unless otherwise noted.

Layout Diagram

Diagram shows finished measurements

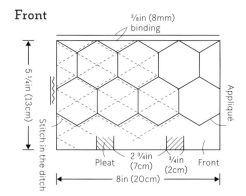

Front

3/8in (8mm) binding

5 ¼in (13cm)

Stitch in the ditch

Appliqué

Pleat · 2 ¾in (7cm) · ¾in (2cm) · Front

8in (20cm)

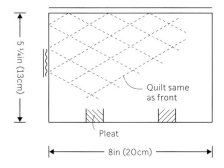

Back

5 ¼in (13cm)

Quilt same as front

Pleat

8in (20cm)

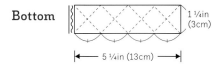

Bottom

1 ¼in (3cm)

5 ¼in (13cm)

Cutting Instructions

Trace and cut out the templates on Pattern Sheet C. Cut out the following fabric pieces, adding ¼in (7mm) seam allowance:

Assorted scraps:
- 13 hexagons

Cut out the following fabric pieces, adding ⅝in (1.5cm) seam allowance:

Main fabric:
- 2 pouches
- 1 bottom

Lining fabric:
- 2 pouches
- 1 bottom

Batting:
- 2 pouches
- 1 bottom

Cut out the following piece, which does not have a template, according to the measurements below (these measurements include seam allowance):

Binding fabric:
- Binding: One 1 ½ x 16 ½in (3.5 x 42cm) single fold bias strip

Construction Steps

1. Sew the 13 hexagons together, starting and stopping at the end of seam marks. Appliqué to the front. Layer the front, batting, and lining. Quilt as shown in the diagram on page 95. Layer the back, batting, and lining. Quilt as shown in the diagram on page 95.

2. Align the front and back with right sides together. Sew together along the sides using ⅝in (1.5cm) seam allowance. On each side, trim the seam allowances, except for one lining layer. Wrap this seam allowance around the others and hemstitch to finish the seam.

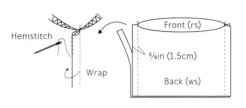

3. Layer the bottom, batting, and lining. Quilt as shown on page 95. Fold and pin the pleats on both the pouch front and back. Using ⅝in (1.5cm) seam allowance, sew the bottom to the pouch with right sides together. Trim the seam allowances, except for the bottom lining. Wrap this seam allowance around the others and hemstitch to finish the seam.

4. Bind the pouch opening, using ¼in (7mm) seam allowances to attach the binding. Sew the zipper to the inside of the pouch as shown.

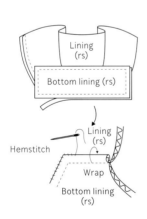

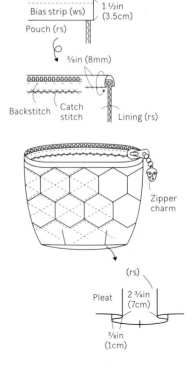

Happy Flower Clutch

Shown on page 21

Materials

- **Appliqué fabric:** Assorted scraps
- **Main fabric:** ⅓yd (0.3m) of polka dot fabric
- **Flap fabric:** ¼yd (0.25m) of print fabric
- **Lining fabric:** ⅓yd (0.3m) of fabric
- **Backing fabric:** ⅓yd (0.3m) of fabric
- **Fusible fleece:** 10 ¾ x 13 ¾in (27 x 35cm)
- 11 ¾in (30cm) of ¼in (5mm) wide lace
- One ⅜in (1cm) magnetic snap set
- No. 25 embroidery floss in brown and dark brown

Layout Diagram

Diagram shows finished measurements

Sew using ¼in (7mm) seam allowance, unless otherwise noted.

Flap

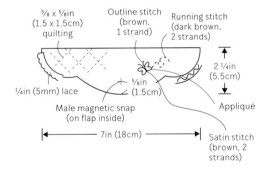

⅝ x ⅝in (1.5 x 1.5cm) quilting

Outline stitch (brown, 1 strand)

Running stitch (dark brown, 2 strands)

2 ¼in (5.5cm)

¼in (5mm) lace

⅝in (1.5cm)

Male magnetic snap (on flap inside)

Appliqué

7in (18cm)

Satin stitch (brown, 2 strands)

Lining

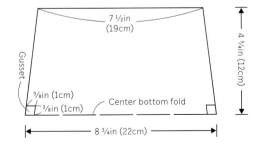

7 ½in (19cm)

Gusset

⅜in (1cm)

⅜in (1cm)

Center bottom fold

4 ¾in (12cm)

8 ¾in (22cm)

Pouch

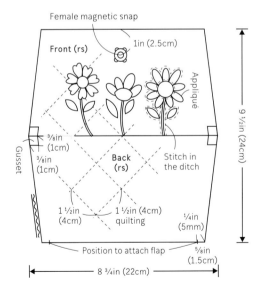

Female magnetic snap

Front (rs)

1in (2.5cm)

Appliqué

Gusset

⅜in (1cm)

⅜in (1cm)

Back (rs)

Stitch in the ditch

1 ½in (4cm)

1 ½in (4cm) quilting

¼in (5mm)

9 ½in (24cm)

Position to attach flap

⅝in (1.5cm)

8 ¾in (22cm)

Cutting Instructions

Trace and cut out the templates on Pattern Sheet C. Cut out the following fabric pieces, adding ¼in (7mm) seam allowance:

Assorted scraps:
- Appliqué pieces

Main fabric:
- 1 front
- 1 back

Flap fabric:
- 1 flap (cut with ⅜in [1cm] seam allowance along top)

Lining fabric:
- 1 flap (cut with ⅜in [1cm] seam allowance along top)

Fusible fleece:
- 1 flap (cut with ⅜in [1cm] seam allowance along top)

Construction Steps

1. Appliqué the floral motif to the front (refer to the template for placement). Sew the front and back together to make the pouch top. Use the assembled pouch top as a template to cut a backing, lining, and piece of fusible fleece. Set the lining aside. Adhere fusible fleece to the wrong side of the assembled top. Align the top and backing with right sides facing out and quilt as shown.

2. Fold the bag in half with right sides together. Sew together along each side.

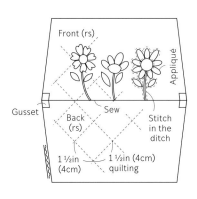

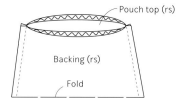

3. To miter each corner, align the side seam with the bottom fold. Mark a line across the corner where it measures ¾in (2cm). Stitch along the marked line.

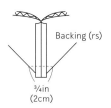

4. Appliqué and embroider the flap. Adhere fusible fleece to the wrong side. Quilt as shown in the diagram on page 97. Sew the flap and lining with right sides together, leaving the top open. Trim the fusible fleece seam allowance and make clips into the curves. Turn right side out. Topstitch the lace to the curved edge.

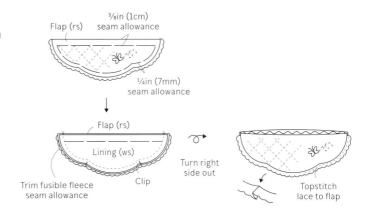

5. Fold the lining in half with right sides together (this was the piece set aside in step 1). Sew together along each side, leaving a 2 ¾in (7cm) opening in one side. With right sides together, insert the pouch into the lining. Sandwich the flap in between so it is aligned with the pouch back (refer to diagram on page 97 for placement). Sew all three layers together around the pouch opening.

6. Turn the pouch right side out through the opening in the lining. Tuck the lining inside the pouch and hemstitch the opening closed. Embroider the bag opening as shown below. Sew the magnetic snap components to the flap inside and pouch front following the placement noted in the diagram on page 97.

Windmill Passport Case

Shown on page 23

Materials

- **Patchwork fabric:** Eleven assorted scraps
- **Lining fabric:** Fat eighth of green floral print fabric
- **Backing fabric:** One fat eighth
- **Pocket A fabric:** Fat quarter of floral print fabric
- **Pocket B fabric:** Fat quarter of floral print fabric
- **Pocket C fabric:** Fat quarter of floral print fabric
- **Pocket D fabric:** Fat quarter of floral print fabric
- **Tab/penholder fabric:** One fat eighth of green floral print fabric
- **Binding fabric:** ½yd (0.5m) of green floral print fabric
- **Batting:** 8 x 10 ¼in (20 x 26cm)
- **Fusible interfacing:** 1 ¼yds (1.2m)
- 15 ¾in (40cm) of ⅜in (1cm) wide lace
- 3 ¼in (8cm) of ⅝in (1.5cm) wide lace
- One ⅜in (1cm) magnetic snap set

Layout Diagram

Diagram shows finished measurements

Sew using ¼in (7mm) seam allowance, unless otherwise noted.

Case Outside

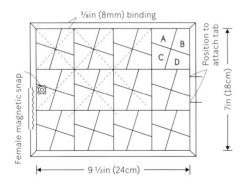

⅜in (8mm) binding

Position to attach tab

A B
C D

7in (18cm)

Female magnetic snap

9 ½in (24cm)

Case Inside

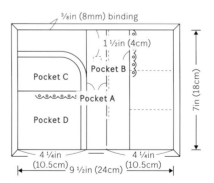

⅜in (8mm) binding

1 ½in (4cm)

Pocket C

Pocket B

Pocket A

Pocket D

7in (18cm)

4 ¼in (10.5cm)   4 ¼in (10.5cm)

9 ½in (24cm)

Pocket B   **Pocket A**

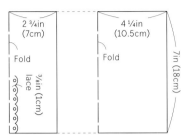

2 ¾in (7cm)

4 ¼in (10.5cm)

Fold

Fold

⅜in (1cm) lace

7in (18cm)

Pocket C

⅜in (8mm) binding

6in (15cm)

4 ¼in (10.5cm)

Pocket D

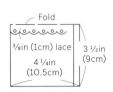

Fold

⅜in (1cm) lace

4 ¼in (10.5cm)

3 ½in (9cm)

Tab

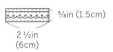

1 ½in (4cm)

⅝in (1.5cm) lace

2 ½in (6.5cm)

Penholder

⅝in (1.5cm)

2 ½in (6cm)

Cutting Instructions

Trace and cut out the templates on Pattern Sheet C. Cut out the following fabric pieces, adding ¼in (7mm) seam allowance:

Assorted scraps:
- 12 A pieces
- 12 B pieces
- 12 C pieces
- 12 D pieces

Tab/penholder fabric:
- 1 penholder
- 1 tab

Pocket A fabric:
- 2 of Pocket A

Pocket B fabric:
- 1 Pocket B

Pocket C fabric:
- 2 of Pocket C

Pocket D fabric:
- 1 Pocket D

Fusible interfacing:
- 1 penholder
- 2 of Pocket A
- 1 Pocket B
- 2 of Pocket C
- 1 Pocket D
- 1 tab

Cut out the following pieces, which do not have templates, according to the measurements below (these measurements include seam allowance):

Backing fabric:
- Backing: 7 ½ x 10in (19.4 x 25.4cm)

Lining fabric:
- Case lining: 7 ½ x 10in (19.4 x 25.4cm)

Fusible interfacing:
- Case lining: 7 ½ x 10in (19.4 x 25.4cm)

Binding fabric:
- Bias binding: 1 ½yds (1.4m) of 1 ½in (3.5cm) wide single fold bias tape

Construction Steps

1. Sew the patchwork pieces A–D together to make 12 blocks (refer to the photo on page 23 for fabric layout).

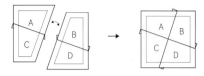

2. Sew the blocks together into three rows of four. Sew the rows together to create the top. Layer the top, batting, and backing. Quilt as shown.

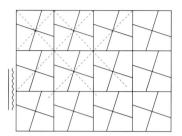

3. Adhere fusible interfacing to the wrong side of the case lining. To make the penholder, adhere fusible interfacing to the wrong side of the penholder piece. Topstitch a piece of lace to the right side, then topstitch along the long edges. Overlap the short edges ⅜in (1cm) and sew to form a loop. Hemstitch the penholder to the lining following placement noted in the diagram.

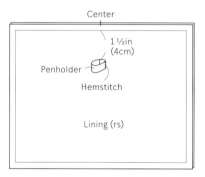

Center

1 ½in (4cm)

Penholder

Hemstitch

Lining (rs)

How to Make the Penholder

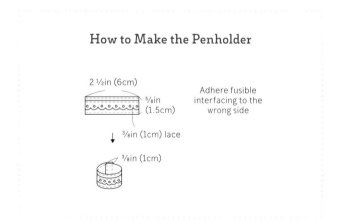

2 ½in (6cm)

⅝in (1.5cm)

Adhere fusible interfacing to the wrong side

⅜in (1cm) lace

⅜in (1cm)

4. To make Pocket A, adhere fusible interfacing to the wrong side and then fold in half. Repeat to make another Pocket A.

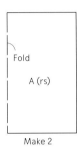

Fold

A (rs)

Make 2

5. To make Pocket B, adhere fusible interfacing to the wrong side and then fold in half. Topstitch a piece of lace to the folded edge.

B (rs)

Fold

³⁄₈in (1cm) lace

6. To make Pocket C, adhere fusible interfacing to the wrong side of each piece. Pin the two pieces with wrong sides together, then set aside.

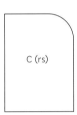

C (rs)

7. To make Pocket D, adhere fusible interfacing to the wrong side and then fold in half. Topstitch a piece of lace to the folded edge.

Fold

³⁄₈in (1cm) lace

D (rs)

8. Align Pocket D on top of Pocket C, matching the raw edges along the bottom. Bind the curved edge (refer to pages 33–34).

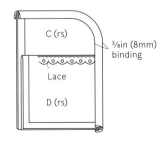

C (rs)

³⁄₈in (8mm) binding

Lace

D (rs)

9. Align Pocket B on top of one Pocket A, matching the raw edges along the right side. Topstitch to divide Pocket B into three equal sections. Topstitch Pocket A, stitching as close to the folded edge as possible.

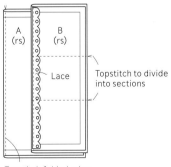

A (rs)

B (rs)

Lace

Topstitch to divide into sections

Topstitch folded edge

10. Topstitch the remaining Pocket A, stitching as closed to the folded edge as possible. Align Pocket C/D on top of Pocket A, matching the raw edges along the left side.

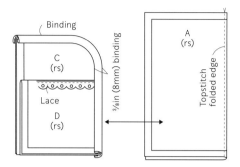

11. Pin the piece from step 10 to the left edge of the lining and the piece from step 9 to the right edge. Align the case top and lining with wrong sides together. Baste around all four edges.

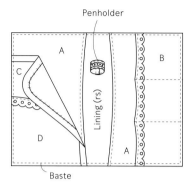

12. Make the tab as shown in the diagram and sew to the right side of the case (refer to diagram on page 100 for placement). Sew the male magnetic snap to the inside of the tab. Bind the case.

Case Inside

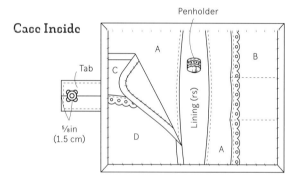

13. Sew the female magnetic snap to the outside of the case.

Case Outside

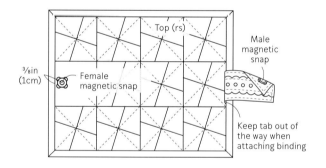

How to Make the Tab

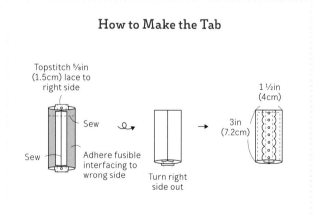

3-D Appliqué Mini Purse

Shown on page 13

Materials

- **Appliqué fabric:** Assorted scraps

- **Main fabric:** ⅓yd (0.3m) of green floral print fabric

- **Backing fabric:** One fat eighth

- **Lining fabric:** One fat quarter

- **Fusible fleece:** 8 x 11 ¾in (20 x 30cm)

- **Fusible interfacing:** 1 ¼ x 47 ¼in (3 x 120cm)

- 14 ¼in (36cm) of ⅜in (8mm) wide lace

- Two ½in (1.2cm) lace flowers

- Two ⅜in (8mm) covered buttons

- One ¾in (2cm) circle of hook and loop tape

- Two ⅝in (1.4cm) jumprings

- Four ½in (1.3cm) swivel hooks

- Two 1/16in (2mm) beads

- No. 8 pearl cotton in blue and variegated yellow

Layout Diagram

Diagram shows finished measurements

Sew using ¼in (7mm) seam allowance, unless otherwise noted.

Body

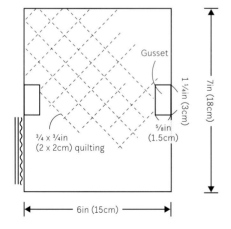

Gusset

1 ¼in (3cm)

7in (18cm)

⅝in (1.5cm)

¾ x ¾in (2 x 2cm) quilting

6in (15cm)

Flap

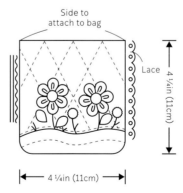

Side to attach to bag

Lace

4 ¼in (11cm)

4 ¼in (11cm)

Handle

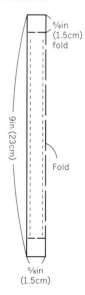

⅝in (1.5cm) fold

9in (23cm)

Fold

⅝in (1.5cm)

Strap

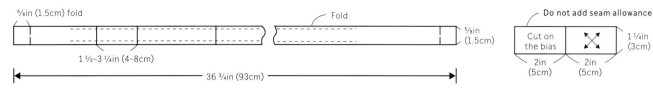

⅝in (1.5cm) fold

1 ½–3 ¼in (4–8cm)

Fold

⅝in (1.5cm)

36 ¾in (93cm)

Loops

Do not add seam allowance

Cut on the bias

1 ¼in (3cm)

2in (5cm)   2in (5cm)

Cutting Instructions

Trace and cut out the templates on Pattern Sheet C. Cut out the following fabric pieces, adding ¼in (7mm) seam allowance, unless otherwise noted:

Assorted scraps:
- Appliqué pieces
- 1 flap
- 12 petals

Backing fabric:
- 1 flap

Lining fabric:
- 1 flap
- 1 body (cut with ⅝in [1.5cm] seam allowance)

Main fabric:
- 1 body

Fusible fleece:
- 1 flap
- 1 body

Cut out the following pieces, which do not have templates, according to the measurements below (these measurements include seam allowance):

Main fabric:
- Loops (cut 2 on the bias): 1 ¼ x 2in (3 x 5cm)
- Binding: 1yd (1m) of 1in (2.5cm) wide single fold bias binding
- Handle: 1 ⅛ x 10 ¾in (2.9 x 27.4cm)
- Strap: 1 ⅛ x 38 ½in (2.9 x 97.4cm)*

*For a patchwork handle, sew 1 ⅛in (2.9cm) wide x 2–3 ⅝in (5.4–9.4cm) long rectangles together until the handle measures 38 ½in (97.4cm) long.

Construction Steps

1. Appliqué the ground and leaf pieces to the flap (refer to the template for placement). Layer the flap, fusible fleece, and backing. (**Note:** Position the glue side of the fusible fleece against the wrong side of the backing). Quilt as shown.

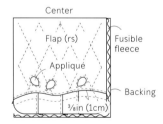

Center

Flap (rs)

Fusible fleece

Appliqué

Backing

⅜in (1cm)

2. Align the flap and lining with right sides together. Sew around three sides, leaving the top open. Press to activate the fusible fleece. Turn right side out. Topstitch the lace to three sides of the flap. Embroider the stems as indicated on the template. Sew the two lace flowers to the flap front, then sew a bead to the center of each lace flower.

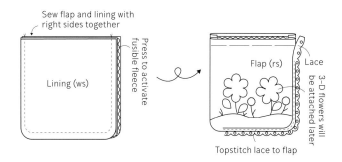

3. Layer the body, fusible fleece, and lining. Quilt as shown.

4. Fold the body in half with right sides together. Sew together along each side using ⅝in (1.5cm) seam allowance. On each side, trim the seam allowances, except for one lining layer. Wrap this seam allowance around the others and hemstitch to finish the seam.

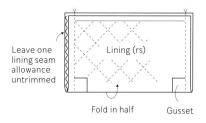

How to Finish the Seam Allowance

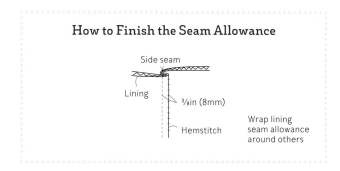

5. To miter each corner, align the side seam with the bottom fold. Mark a line across the corner where it measures 1 ¼in (3cm) wide. Stitch along the marked line. Hemstitch the seam allowance to the bottom of the bag.

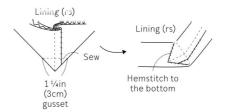

6. Sew the flap to the bag back with right sides together. Make two loops as shown in the diagram. Pin a loop to each bag side seam with the jumpring facing down. Bind the bag opening using the bias strip.

7. Sew the pieces of hook and loop tape to the flap inside and bag front following placement noted below.

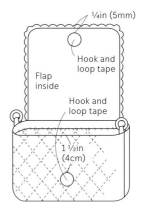

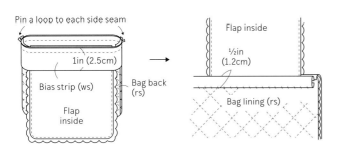

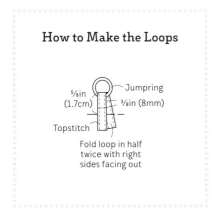

8. To make the handle, fold and press the seam allowances over to the wrong side. Fold each handle in half. Topstitch each long edge. Fold and press each short edge over ¼in (7mm). Thread a swivel hook onto each short edge, then fold over ⅝in (1.5cm). Topstitch the short end to the wrong side of the handle.

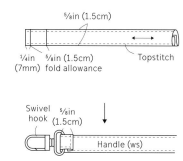

Follow the same process to make the long strap, but sew the pieces together first if creating a patchwork strap.

9. Make two 3-D flowers as shown below.

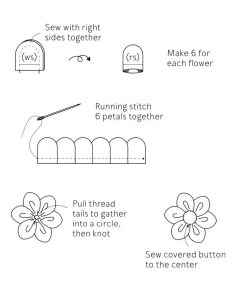

10. Sew the 3-D flowers to the flap front. Clip the handle or the strap to the loops on the bag.

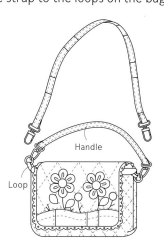

Big Sister Tote

Shown on page 24

Materials

- **Patchwork fabric:** Assorted scraps

- **Bag fabric:** ⅝yd (0.6m) of pre-quilted fabric

- **Lining fabric:** ¾yd (0.7m) of fabric

- **Fusible interfacing:** 5 ½ x 8in (14 x 20cm)

- 1 ½in (4cm) of ⅝in (1.5cm) wide cotton tape

- Two ¾ x 15 ¾in (2 x 40cm) handles

- No. 8 pearl cotton in pink

Layout Diagram

Diagram shows finished measurements

Sew using ¼in (7mm) seam allowance, unless otherwise noted.

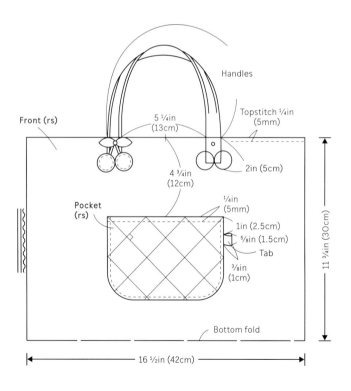

Cutting Instructions

Trace and cut out the templates on Pattern Sheet C. Cut out the following fabric pieces, adding ¼in (7mm) seam allowance:

Assorted scraps:
- Patchwork pieces

Lining fabric:
- 1 pocket

Fusible interfacing:
- 1 pocket (do not add seam allowance)

Cut out the following pieces, which do not have templates, according to the measurements below (these measurements include seam allowance):

Bag fabric:
- Bag: 17 x 24in (43.4 x 61.4cm)

Lining fabric:
- Lining: 17 x 24in (43.4 x 61.4cm)
- Handle supports (cut 4): 2 x 2 ¼in (4.9 x 5.9cm)

Construction Steps

1. To make the pocket top, sew the patchwork pieces together as shown. Use the pocket template to trim the patchwork into shape, leaving ¼in (7mm) seam allowance.

2. Fold the cotton tape in half and baste the short edges together to make the tab. Adhere fusible interfacing to the wrong side of the pocket lining. Align the pocket and lining with right sides together with the tab sandwiched in between (refer to the diagram on page 110 for placement). Sew together, leaving a 2 ½in (6cm) opening along the bottom.

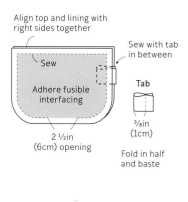

Align top and lining with right sides together

Sew with tab in between

Sew

Adhere fusible interfacing

Tab

2 ½in (6cm) opening

⅜in (1cm)

Fold in half and baste

Sew

Sew

Trace template

Pocket template

Pocket top

3. Turn the pocket right side out and topstitch the upper edge using ¼in (5mm) seam allowance.

4. Topstitch the pocket to the bag following placement noted in the diagram below.

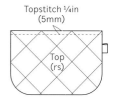

Topstitch ¼in (5mm)

Top (rs)

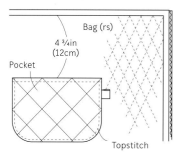

Bag (rs)

4 ¾in (12cm)

Pocket

Topstitch

5. Align the bag and lining with right sides together. Sew together along the upper and lower edges. Press the seams open.

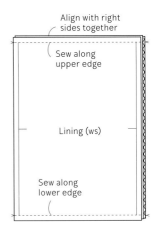

6. Align the bag so that the seams from step 5 are positioned at the center. Sew along the left and right edges, leaving a 4in (10cm) opening in one edge. Press the seams open.

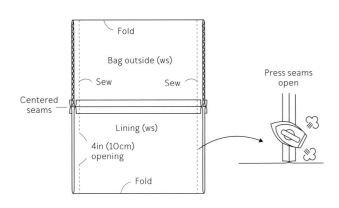

7. Turn right side out. Tuck the lining inside the bag and hemstitch the opening closed. Topstitch the bag along the opening using ¼in (5mm) seam allowance.

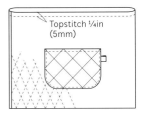

8. Backstitch the handles to the bag (refer to the diagram on page 110 for placement). Handstitch the support fabric to the lining to cover the stitching from attaching the handles.

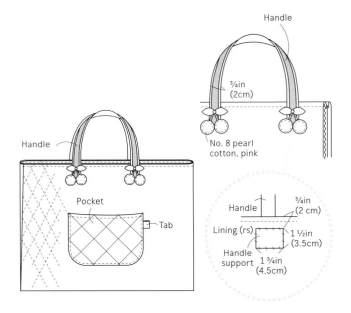

Little Sister Tote

Shown on page 24

Materials

- **Patchwork fabric:** Assorted scraps

- **Bag fabric:** ⅓yd (0.3m) of pre-quilted fabric

- **Lining fabric:** ⅓yd (0.3m) of fabric

- **Handle support fabric:** 6in (15cm) square scrap

- One ¾in (2cm) circle of hook and loop tape

- Two ¾ x 15 ¾in (2 x 40cm) handles

- No. 8 pearl cotton in pink

Layout Diagram

Diagram shows finished measurements

Sew using ¼in (7mm) seam allowance, unless otherwise noted.

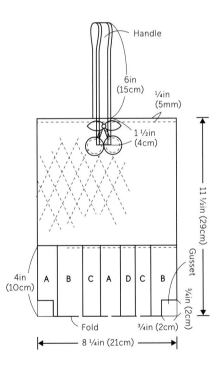

Cutting Instructions

Trace and cut out the templates on Pattern Sheet C. Cut out the following fabric pieces, adding ¼in (7mm) seam allowance:

Assorted scraps:
- 2 A pieces
- 2 B pieces
- 2 C pieces
- 1 D piece

Cut out the following pieces, which do not have templates, according to the measurements below (these measurements include seam allowance):

Bag fabric:
- Bag: 8 ¾ x 23 ½in (22.4 x 59.4cm)

Lining fabric:
- Lining: 8 ¾ x 23 ½in (22.4 x 59.4cm)

Handle support fabric:
- Handle supports (cut 4): 2 x 2 ¼in (4.9 x 5.9cm)

Construction Steps

1. Sew the patchwork pieces together following the layout shown in the diagram on page 113. Fold and press the upper and lower seam allowances under. Topstitch to the bag following placement noted in the diagram on page 113.

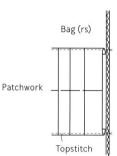

2. Align the bag and lining with right sides together. Sew together along the upper and lower edges. Press the seams open.

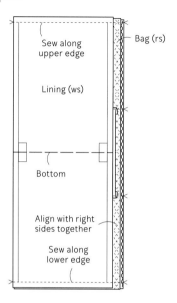

3. Align the bag so that the seams from step 2 are positioned at the center. Sew along the left and right edges, leaving a 4in (10cm) opening in one edge. Press the seams open. To miter each corner, align each side seam with the fold. Mark a line across the corner where it measures 1 ½in (4cm). Stitch along the marked line.

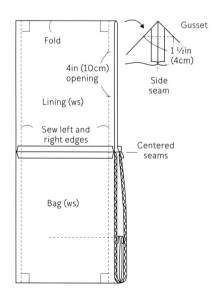

4. Turn right side out. Tuck the lining inside the bag and hemstitch the opening closed. Topstitch the bag along the opening using ¼in (5mm) seam allowance. Backstitch the handles to the bag (refer to the diagram on page 113 for placement). Handstitch the support fabric to the lining to cover the stitching from attaching the handles, as shown on page 112. Sew the pieces of hook and loop tape to the inside of the bag following placement noted below.

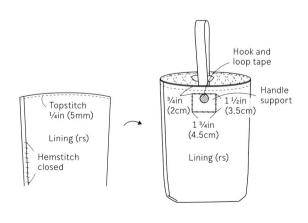

Lovely Vines Quilt

Shown on page 22

Materials

- **Patchwork and appliqué fabric:** Assorted scraps, including a selection of assorted green scraps

- **Background fabric:** 3yds (2.8m) of white fabric

- **Accent fabric:** 2yds (1.9m) of solid green fabric

- **Border fabric:** 2yds (1.9m) of green floral print fabric

- **Backing fabric:** 4 ½yds (4.2m) of fabric

- **Batting:** 71 x 87in (180 x 220cm)

Layout Diagram

Diagram shows finished measurements

Sew using ¼in (7mm) seam allowance, unless otherwise noted.

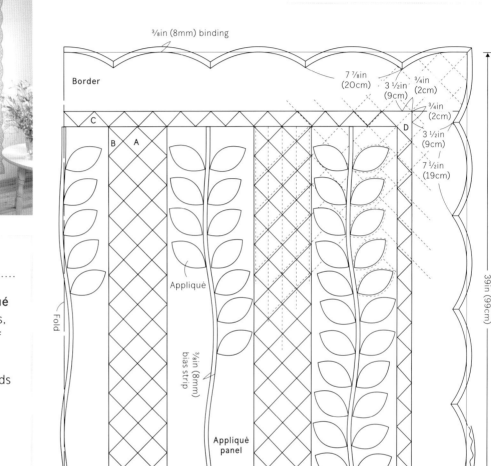

Cutting Instructions

Trace and cut out the templates on Pattern Sheet D. Cut out the following fabric pieces, adding ¼in (7mm) seam allowance:

Assorted scraps:
- 344 A squares
- 260 leaves

Accent fabric:
- 224 B triangles

Background fabric:
- 98 C triangles
- 4 D triangles

Green assorted scraps:
- 102 C triangles

Cut out the following pieces, which do not have templates, according to the measurements below (these measurements include seam allowance):

Accent fabric:
- Vines: 9 ¼yds (8.4m) of 1 ½in (3.5cm) wide single fold bias binding
- Binding: 8yds (7.4m) of 1 ½in (3.5cm) wide single fold bias binding

Main fabric:
- Appliqué panels (cut 5): 7 ½ x 70in (19.4 x 178cm)

Border fabric:
- Side borders (cut 2): 5 ¼ x 69in (13.4 x 175.4cm)
- Top/bottom borders (cut 2): 5 ¼ x 66 ½in (13.4 x 169.4cm)

Construction Steps

1. Piece 86 A squares and 56 B triangles together to make one patchwork panel (refer to Figure 1 on page 117). Repeat to make three more panels.

2. Cut a 70in (178cm) long piece of the vine bias binding. Fold in half lengthwise with wrong sides together and press. Pin the vine in place following the placement noted in the diagram on page 115. Sew the raw edges down using a ¼in (7mm) seam. Fold the remaining edge over the seam allowance, pin in place, and hand sew the folded edge to the appliqué panel (refer to Figure 2 on page 117).

3. Appliqué 52 leaves to the vine, following the placement noted in the diagram on page 115 (also refer to Figure 3 on page 117).

4. Repeat steps 2 and 3 to make a total of five appliquéd panels

5. Trim the appliquéd panels to measure 7 ½ x 66 ½in (19.4 x 169.4cm).

6. Sew the appliquéd and patchwork panels together.

7. Piece 27 white and 28 green C triangles together to make one side patchwork border. Sew the side border to the quilt. Repeat for the other side. Then piece 22 white and 23 green C triangles together to make one top patchwork border. Sew the top border to the quilt. Repeat for the bottom. Finally, sew a D triangle to each corner of the quilt.

8. Follow the method used in steps 4 and 5 on page 41 to calculate the outer border lengths. Sew the side borders to the quilt, then add the top and bottom borders.

9. Piece the backing together as necessary. Layer the top, batting, and backing. Quilt as shown in Figure 4 on page 117).

10. Use the template on Pattern Sheet D to mark and cut the border scallops and corners. Make sure to align the corner of the template with the corner of the quilt. The first scallop on each side should end ¾in (2cm) from the corner of the D triangle.

11. Bind the quilt (refer to pages 33–34).

Figure 1: How to Make the Patchwork Panels

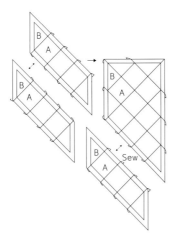

Figure 3: How to Appliqué the Leaves

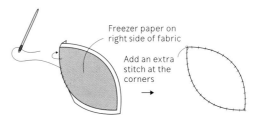

Freezer paper on right side of fabric

Add an extra stitch at the corners

Figure 2: How to Appliqué the Vines

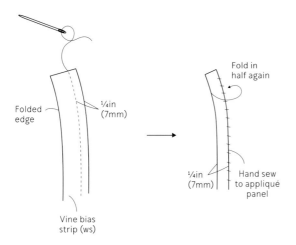

Folded edge

¼in (7mm)

Fold in half again

¼in (7mm)

Hand sew to appliqué panel

Vine bias strip (ws)

Figure 4: How to Quilt

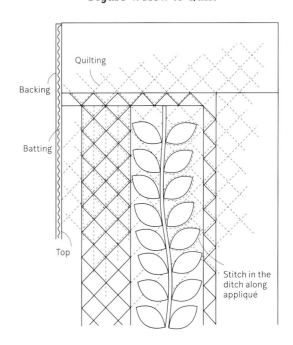

Quilting

Backing

Batting

Top

Stitch in the ditch along appliqué

Happy Flower Quilt Sampler

Shown on page 25

Materials

- **Patchwork and appliqué fabric.** Assorted scraps

- **Sashing fabric:** 1 ¼yds (1.2m) of solid pink fabric

- **Border fabric:** 2yds (1.9m) of pink plaid fabric

- **Backing fabric:** 4 ½yds (4m) of fabric

- **Binding fabric:** ½yd (0.5m) of pink fabric

- **Batting:** 67 x 78¾in (170 x 200cm)

- No. 25 embroidery floss in assorted colors

Layout Diagram
Diagram shows finished measurements

Sew using ¼in (7mm) seam allowance, unless otherwise noted.

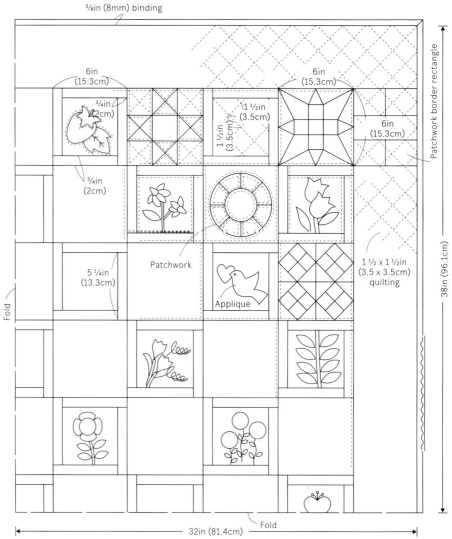

Cutting Instructions

Trace and cut out the templates on pages 121–143 and Pattern Sheet D. Cut out the following fabric pieces, adding ¼in (7mm) seam allowance to the appliqué pieces only:

Assorted scraps:
- Patchwork and appliqué pieces for 91 blocks

Cut out the following pieces, which do not have templates, according to the measurements below (these measurements include seam allowance):

Assorted scraps:
- Fussy cut blocks (cut 8): 5in (12.7cm) squares
- Appliqué block backgrounds (cut 41): 5in (12.7cm) squares
- Patchwork border rectangles (cut 18): 2 ½ x 3in (6.4 x 7.7cm)

Sashing fabric:
- Sashing rectangles (cut 196): 1 ¼ x 5 ¾in (3.4 x 14.7cm)

Border fabric:
- Patchwork border rectangles (cut 18): 2 ½ x 3in (6.4 x 7.7cm)
- Border A: 5 ½ x 18 ¼in (13.9 x 46.4cm)
- Border B: 5 ½ x 35in (13.9 x 88.9cm)
- Border C: 5 ½ x 36in (13.9 x 91.4cm)
- Border D: 5 ½ x 23 ⅛in (13.9 x 58.9cm)
- Border E: 5 ½ x 24 ⅛in (13.9 x 61.4cm)
- Border F: 5 ½ x 29in (13.9 x 73.9cm)

Binding fabric:
- Binding: 7 ¾yds (7m) of 1 ½in (3.5cm) wide single fold bias binding

Construction Steps

1. Use the templates on pages 121–143 to make 50 patchwork blocks with an unfinished size of 6 ½in (16.7cm).

2. Use the templates on Pattern Sheet D to make 41 appliqué blocks with an unfinished size of 5in (12.7cm). Use partial seams to sew four sashing rectangles to each block. The sashed block will have an unfinished size of 6 ½in (16.7cm).

3. Make eight fussy cut blocks using the 5in (12.7cm) squares and sashing rectangles. The unfinished size of these blocks will be 6 ½in (16.7cm).

4. Sew the 99 blocks together into 11 rows of nine blocks each, alternating sashed and non-sashed blocks (refer to the photo on page 25 for layout).

5. Sew three assorted scrap and three border fabric rectangles together to make a border patchwork block. Make five more.

6. Follow the method used in steps 4 and 5 on page 41 to calculate the total border lengths. Refer to Figure 1 to piece the border strips and patchwork border blocks together. Use partial seams to sew the four borders to the quilt.

7. Piece the backing together as necessary. Layer the top, batting, and backing. Quilt as shown in the diagram on page 118.

8. Bind the quilt (refer to Figure 2 on page 120).

Figure 1: How to Assemble the Border

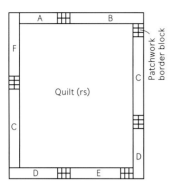

Figure 2: How to Bind the Quilt

1. Cut the bias strips. Sew the bias strips together until they equal desired length.

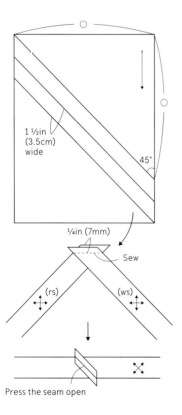

1 ½in (3.5cm) wide

45°

¼in (7mm)

Sew

(rs)   (ws)

Press the seam open

2. Sew the bias binding to the quilt.

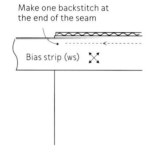

Make one backstitch at the end of the seam

Bias strip (ws)

3. Fold the bias strip up and away from the quilt at a 45° angle. Crease and fold back down so the fold aligns with the edge of the quilt. Continue sewing along the next side of the quilt.

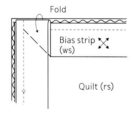

Fold

Bias strip (ws)

Quilt (rs)

4. Fold the bias strip to the back of the quilt and hemstitch.

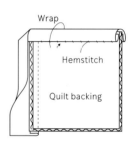

Wrap

Hemstitch

Quilt backing

5. Fold the corner into a miter, then continue hemstitching the bias strip to the back of the quilt.

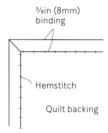

⅜in (8mm) binding

Hemstitch

Quilt backing

Happy Flower Quilt Sampler

Patchwork Templates

All of the patchwork block templates for the Happy Flower Quilt Sampler are included on pages 121–143. The templates on this page are basic triangles common to several different blocks, so use these when referenced in the individual block instructions. Cutting dimensions are provided for square pieces (these measurements include seam allowance).

Triangles

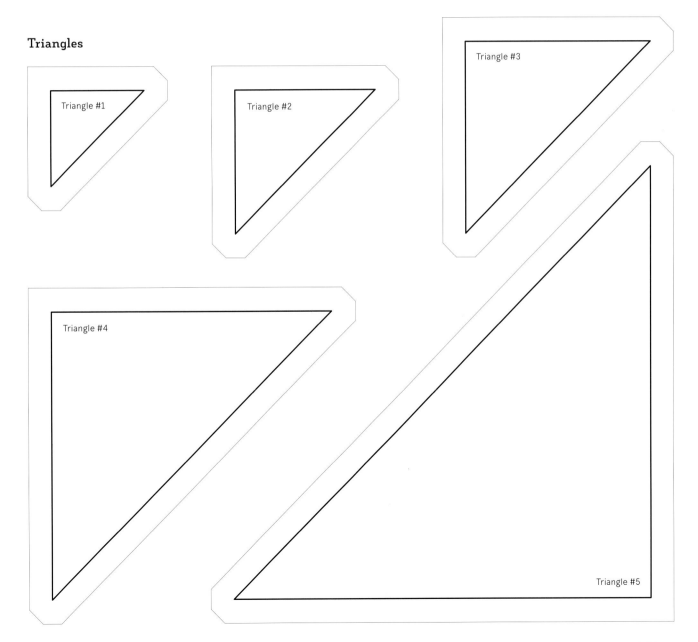

Triangle #1

Triangle #2

Triangle #3

Triangle #4

Triangle #5

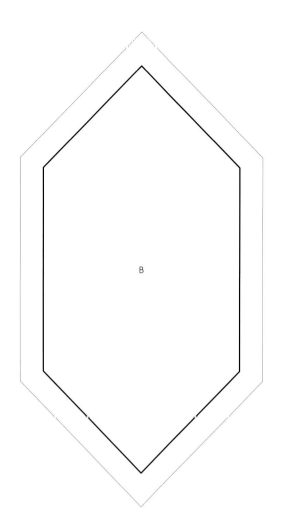

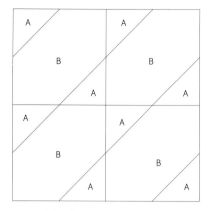

A: Use Triangle #2 on page 121.

Block #7

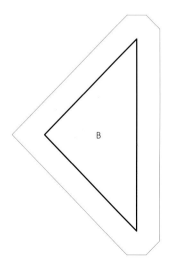

A: Cut 2 ½in (6.5cm) squares.

Block #3

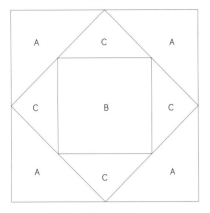

B: Cut a 3 ½in (9cm) square.

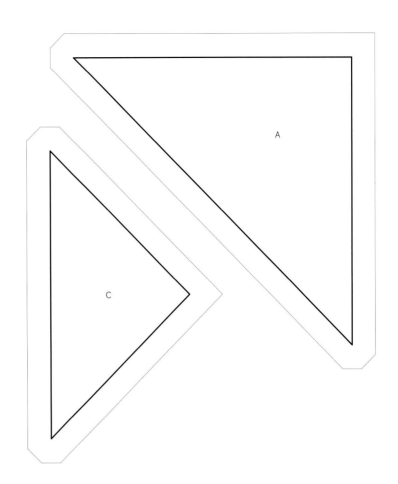

Block #61

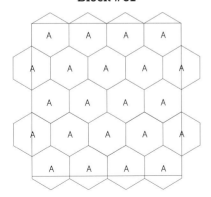

Note: Trim block to 6 ½in (16.7cm) square after assembling hexies as shown.

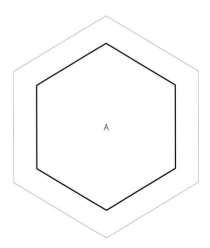

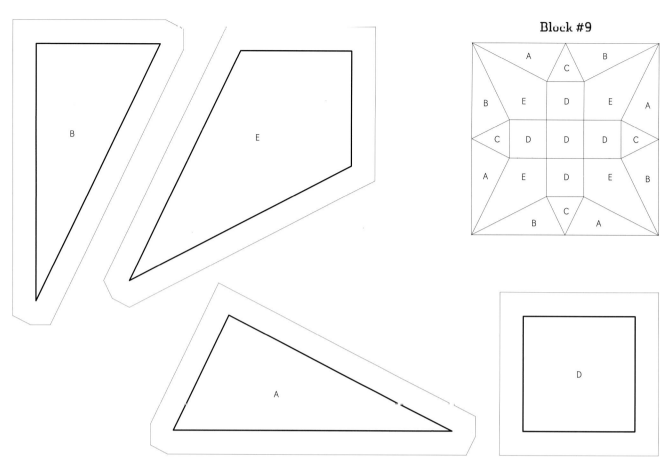

Block #9

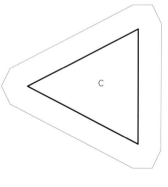

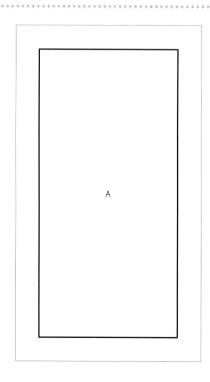

Block #19

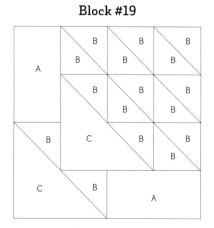

B: Use Triangle #2 on page 121.
C: Use Triangle #4 on page 121.

Block #11

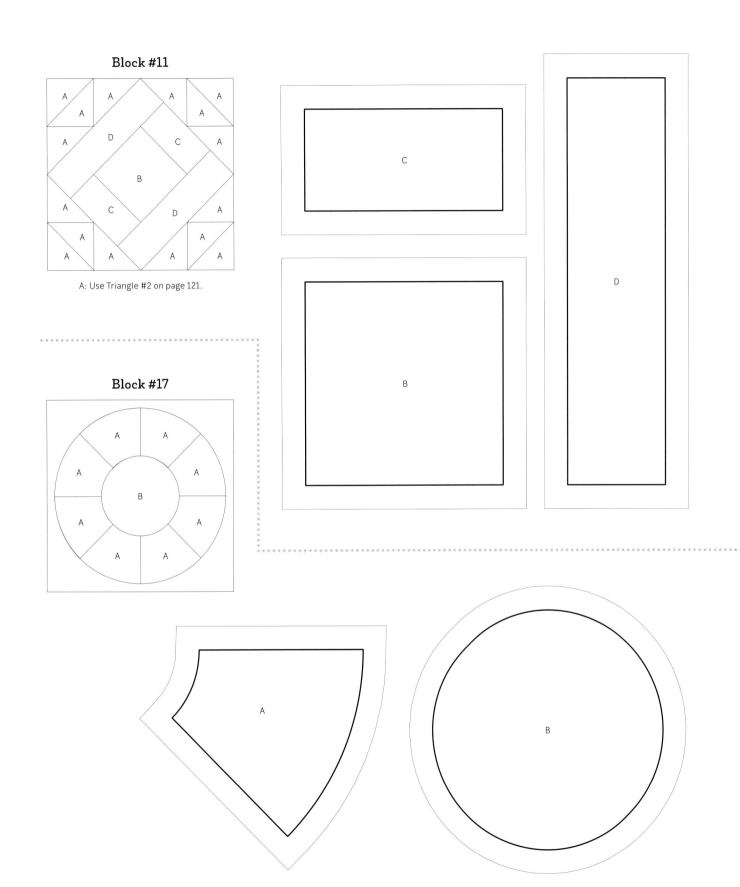

A: Use Triangle #2 on page 121.

Block #17

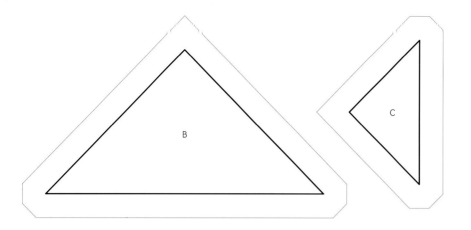

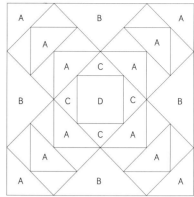

Block #13

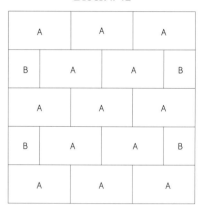

A: Use Triangle #2 on page 121.
D: Cut a 2in (5cm) square.

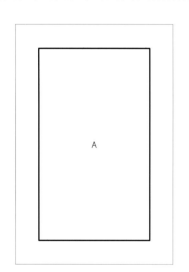

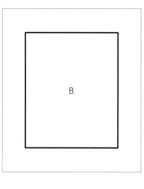

Block #41

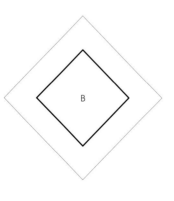

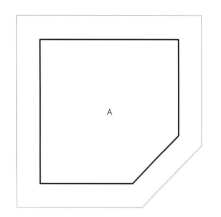

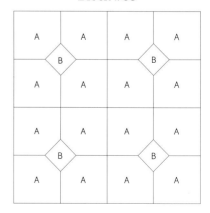

Block #53

Block #21

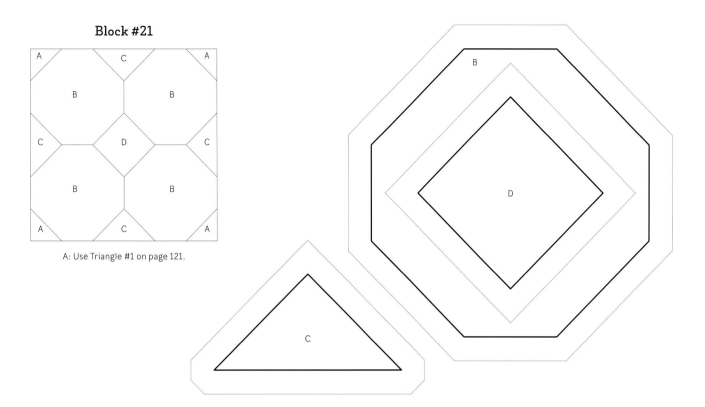

A: Use Triangle #1 on page 121.

Block #45

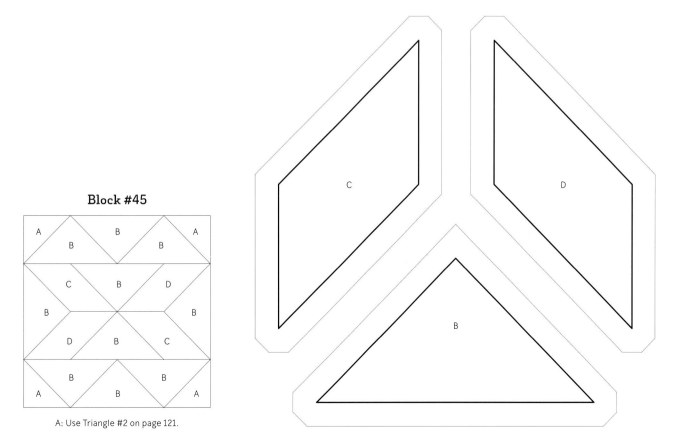

A: Use Triangle #2 on page 121.

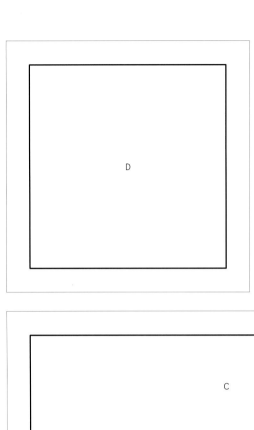

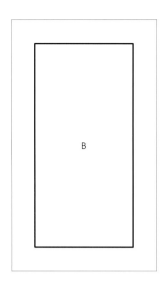

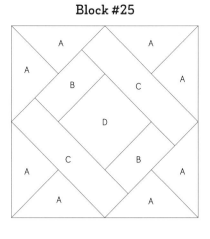

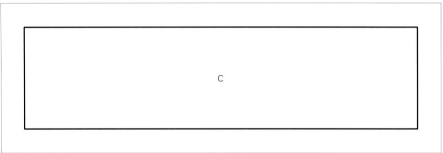

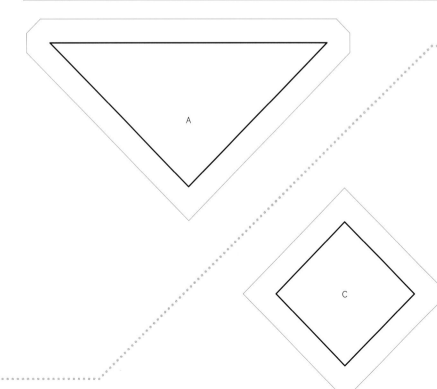

Block #27

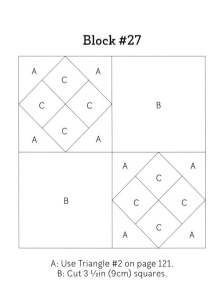

A: Use Triangle #2 on page 121.
B: Cut 3 ½in (9cm) squares.

Block #29

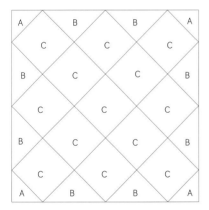

A: Cut 1 ½in (4cm) squares.

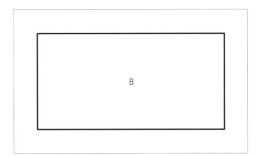

Block #31

A: Use Triangle #1 on page 121.

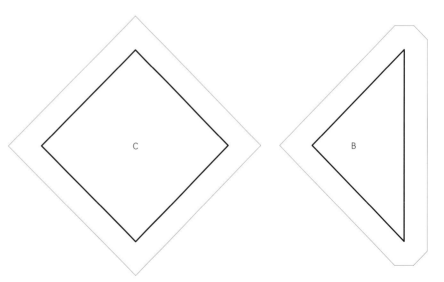

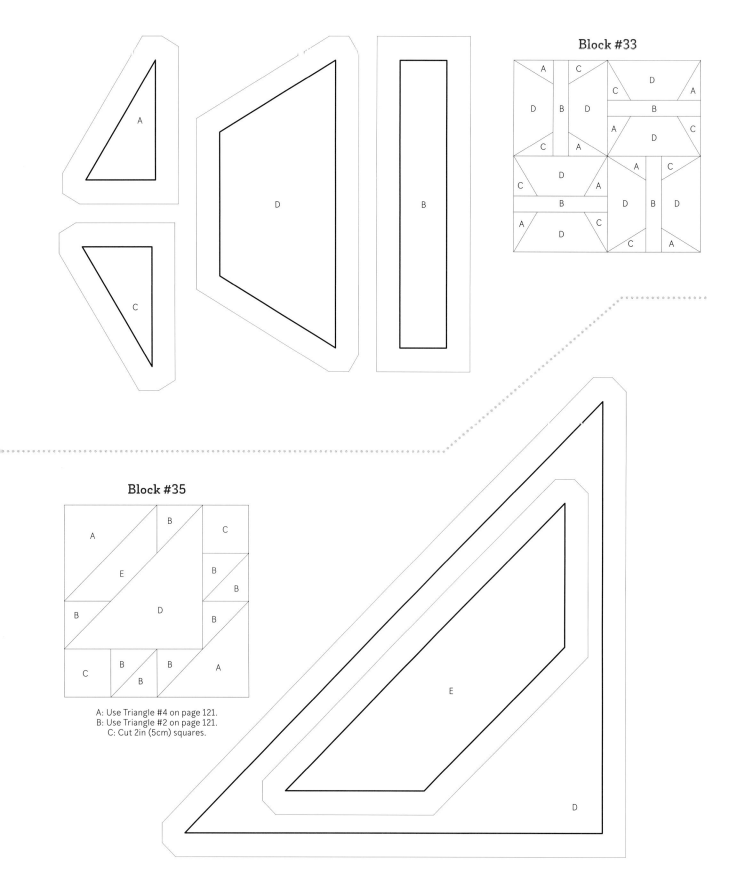

Block #33

Block #35

A: Use Triangle #4 on page 121.
B: Use Triangle #2 on page 121.
C: Cut 2in (5cm) squares.

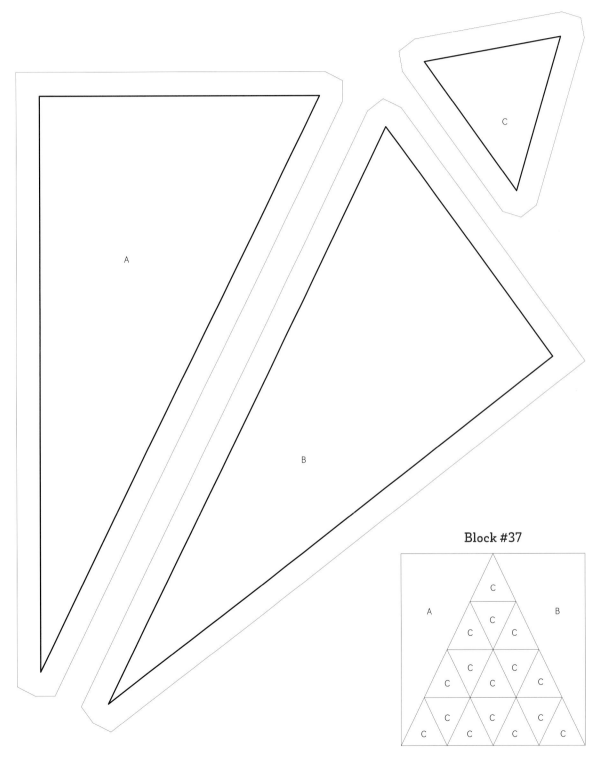

A

B

C

Block #37

C

A   B

C
C   C
C   C
C   C   C
C   C   C
C   C   C

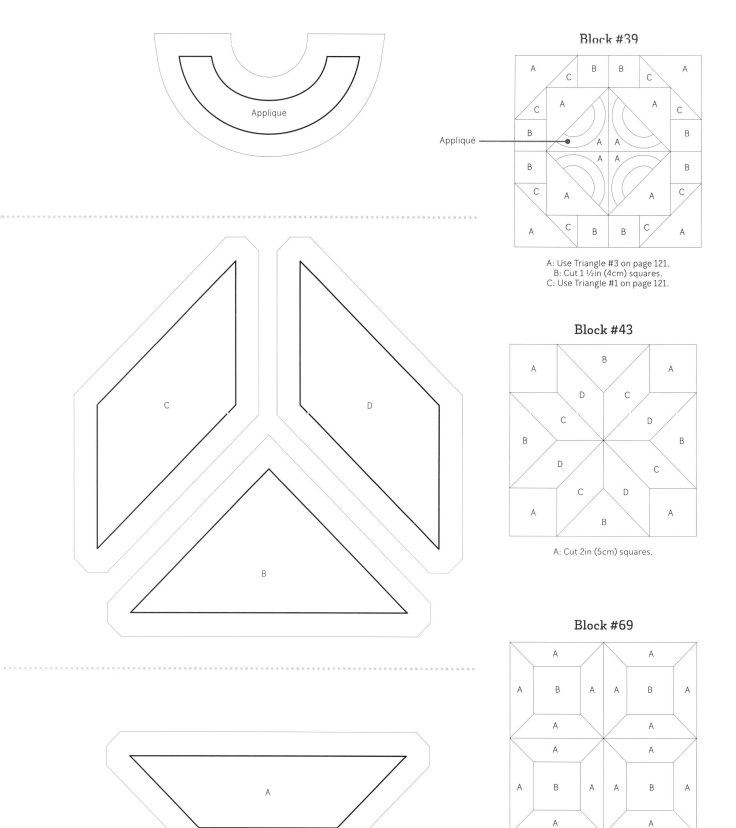

Appliqué

Block #39

A
C
B
B
C
A

C
A
A
C

B
A
A
B

B
A
A
B

C
A
A
C

A
C
B
B
C
A

Appliqué

A: Use Triangle #3 on page 121.
B: Cut 1 ½in (4cm) squares.
C: Use Triangle #1 on page 121.

Block #43

A
B
A

D
C

C
D

B
B

D
C

A
C
D
A

B

A: Cut 2in (5cm) squares.

Block #69

A
A

A
B
A
A
B
A

A
A

A
A

A
B
A
A
B
A

A
A

B: Cut 2in (5cm) squares.

C

D

B

A

Block #47

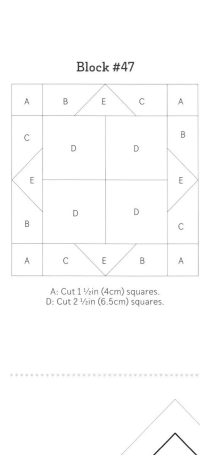

A: Cut 1 ½in (4cm) squares.
D: Cut 2 ½in (6.5cm) squares.

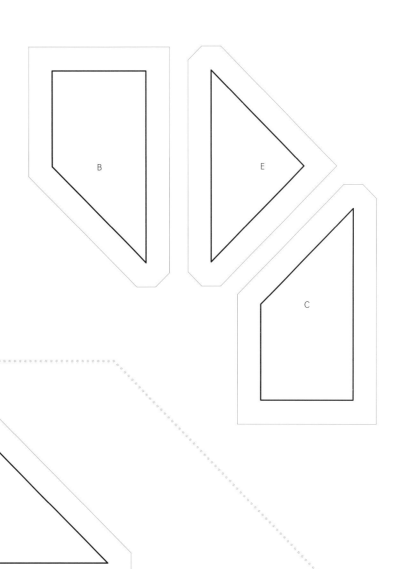

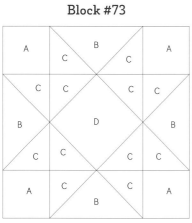

Block #73

A: Cut 2in (5cm) squares.
C: Use Triangle #2 on page 121.

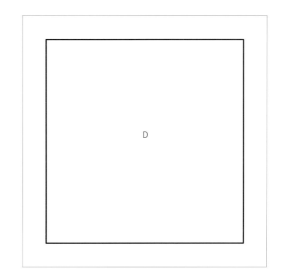

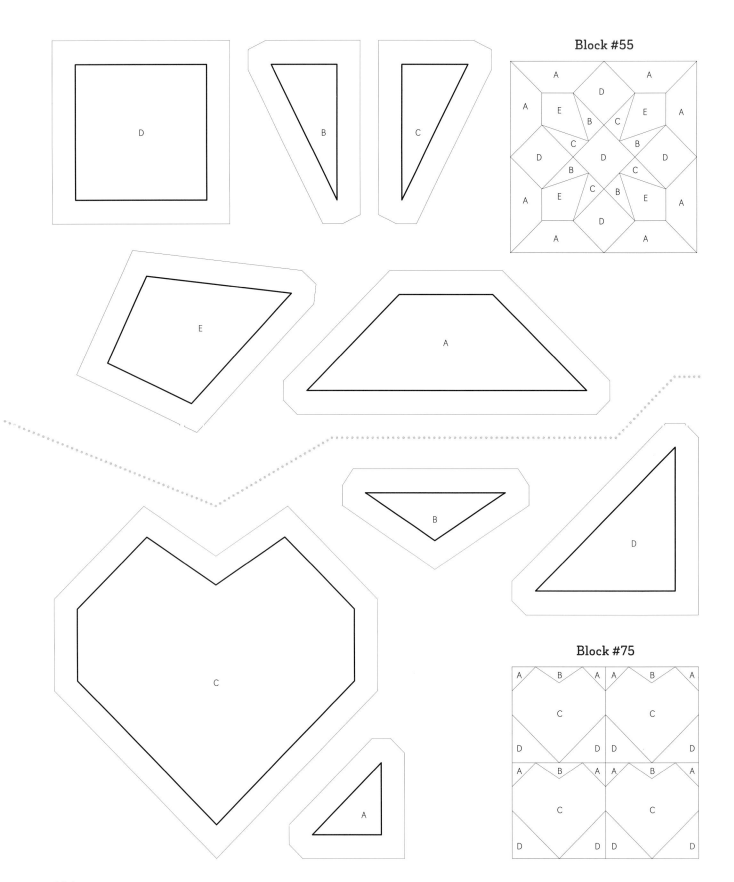

Block #55

Block #75

Block #57

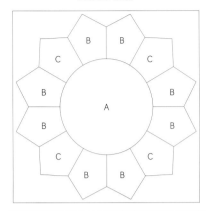

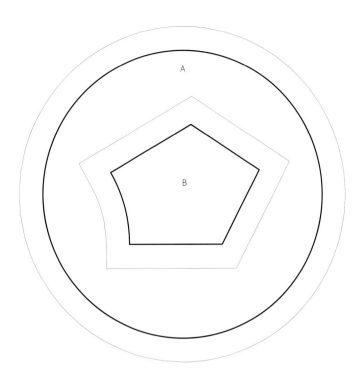

> **Note:** Appliqué the flower to a 6 ½in (16.7cm) square background.

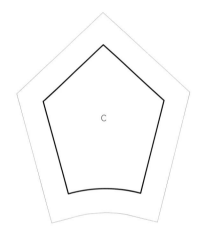

Block #5

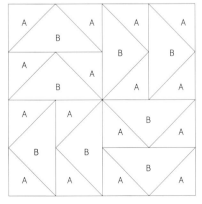

A: Use Triangle #2 on page 121.

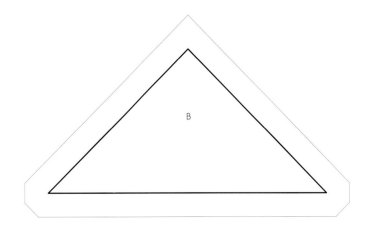

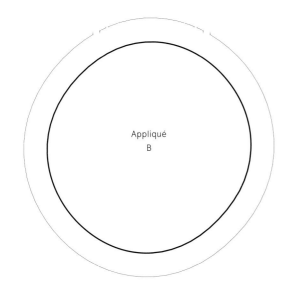

Block #81

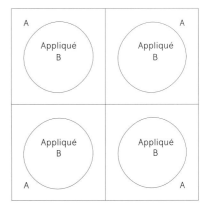

A: Cut 3 ½in (9cm) squares.

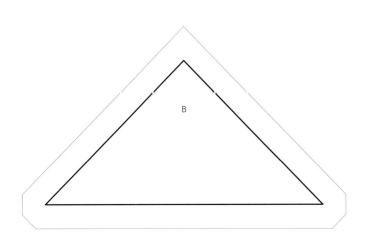

Block #89

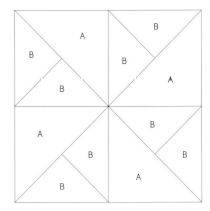

A: Use Triangle #4 on page 121.

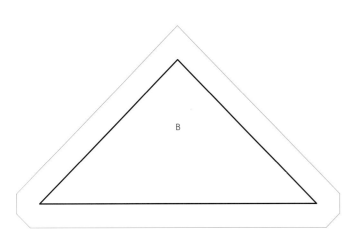

Block #71

A: Cut 2in (5cm) squares.
C: Use Triangle #2 on page 121.
D: Cut a 3 ½in (9cm) square.

Block #65

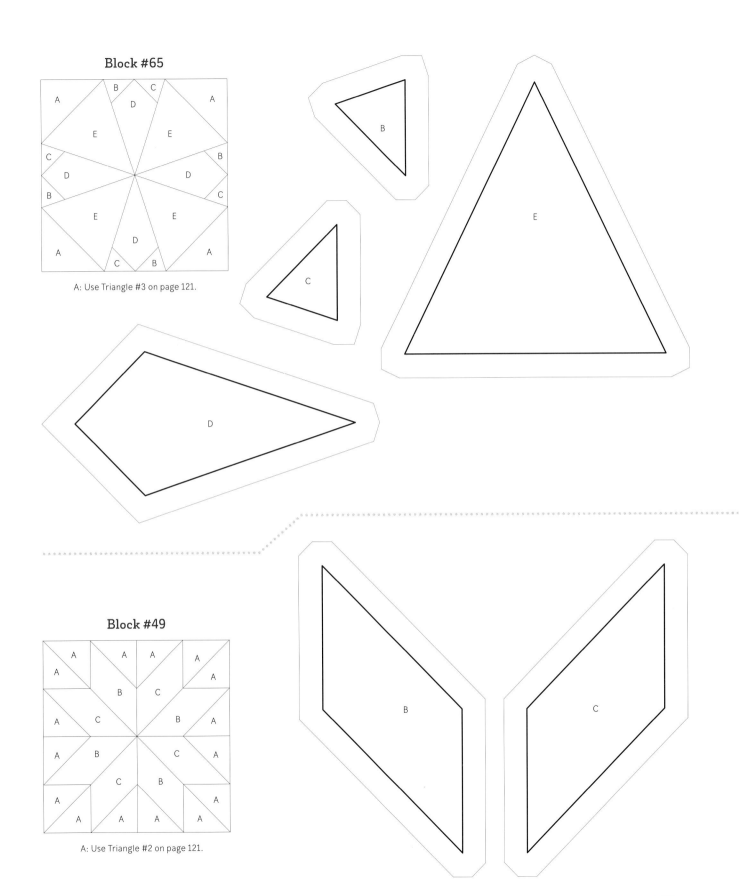

A: Use Triangle #3 on page 121.

Block #49

A: Use Triangle #2 on page 121.

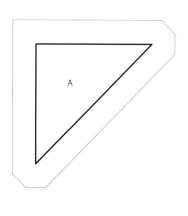

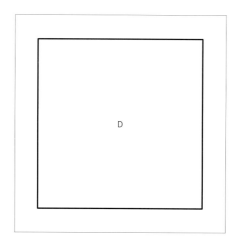

Block #95

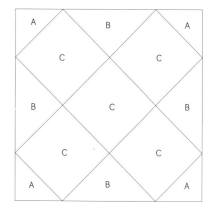

C: Cut a 1 ½in (4cm) square.

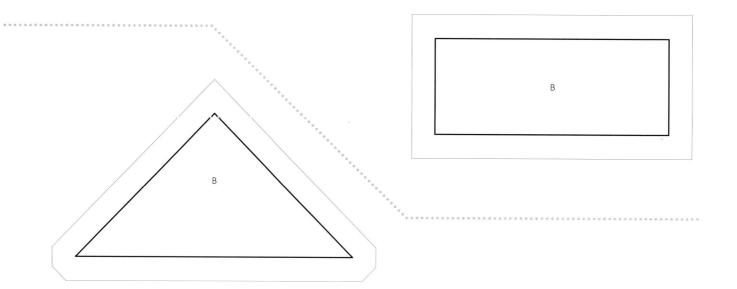

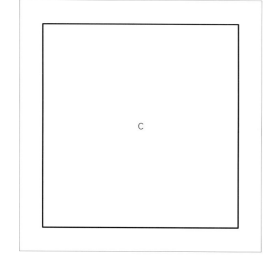

Block #93

A: Use Triangle #2 on page 121.

Block #79

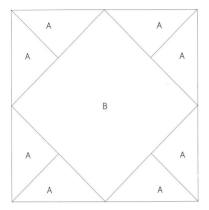

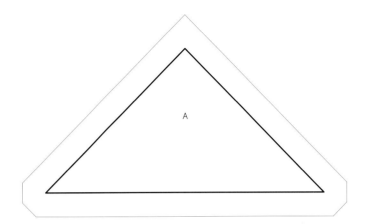

A

B

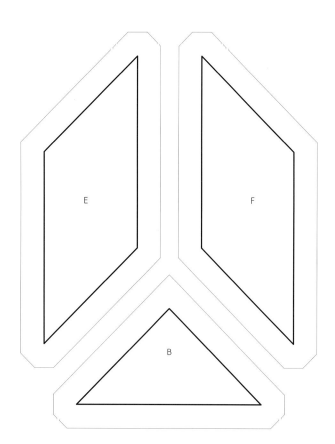

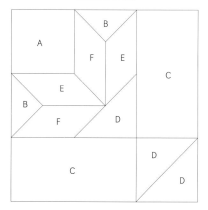

A: Cut a 2 ½in (6.5cm) square.
D: Use Triangle #3 on page 121.

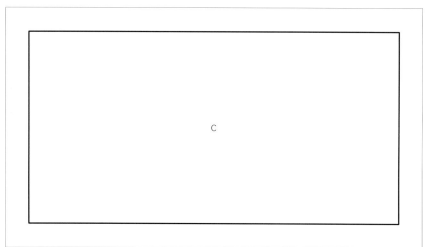

Block #99

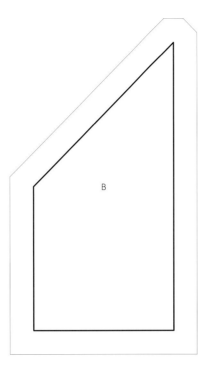
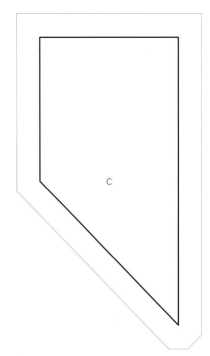

A: Cut 2in (5cm) squares.
D: Use Triangle #2 on page 121.

Block #51

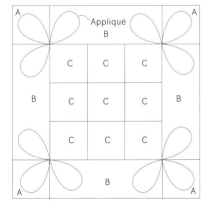
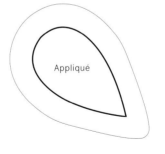
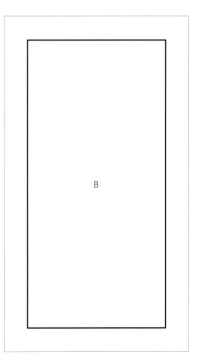

A: Cut 2in (5cm) squares.
C: Cut 1 ½in (4cm) squares.

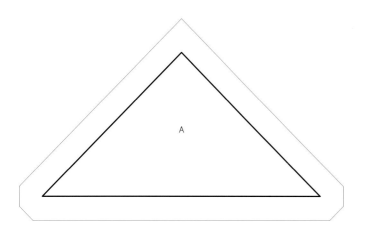

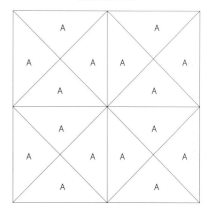

Block #67

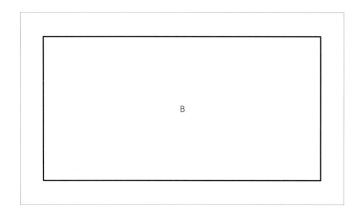

Block #87

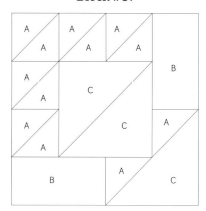

A: Use Triangle #2 on page 121.
C: Use Triangle #4 on page 121.

Block #59

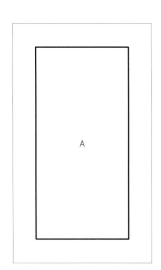

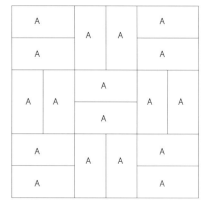

Block #15

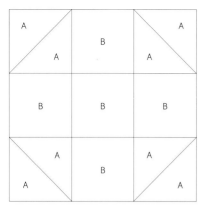

A: Use Triangle #3 on page 121.
B: Cut 2 ½in (6.5cm) squares.

Block #23

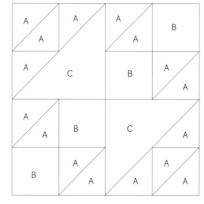

A: Use Triangle #2 on page 121.
B: Cut 2in (5cm) squares.
C: Use Triangle #4 on page 121.

Block #77

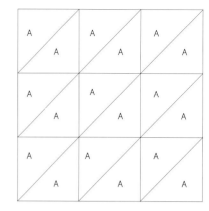

A: Use Triangle #3 on page 121.

Block #83

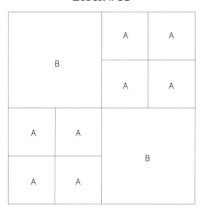

A: Cut 2in (5cm) squares.
B: Cut 3 ½in (9cm) squares.

Block #85

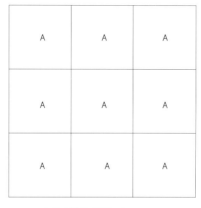

A: Cut 2 ½in (6.5cm) squares.

All templates are full-size.
Use the block illustrations for
layout reference.

Trace or photocopy the templates.
Do not cut this sheet.

Note: Seam allowance is
included for these templates.

Cutting dimensions for squares
include seam allowance.

Block #97

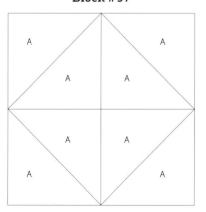

A: Use Triangle #4 on page 121.

Block #63

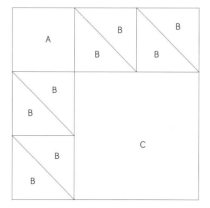

A: Cut a 2 ½in (6.5cm) square.
B: Use Triangle #3 on page 121.
C: Cut a 4 ½in (11.5cm) square.

Resources

A-Two Quilt Studio
www.a-two.com

Atsuko Matsuyama's quilt shop featuring her favorite fabrics, notions, and tools. Shipping within Japan only.

Etsy
www.etsy.com

Many great Etsy shops offer vintage feedsacks, 1930s reproduction fabrics, bag hardware, and zakka-style zippers perfect for making the projects in this book. Ships from sellers based around the world.

Pink Castle Fabrics
www.pinkcastlefabrics.com

Offers a great selection of Atsuko Matsuyama fabric, as well as other retro fabric. Ships from the United States.

Pretty Fabrics and Trims
www.prettyfabricsandtrims.co.uk

Wonderful assortment of 1930s reproduction fabrics, lace trims, and buttons. Ships from the United Kingdom.

Sharon's Antiques Vintage Fabrics
www.rickrack.com

Online emporium for vintage feedsacks and antique textiles. Ships from the United States.

The Homemakery
www.thehomemakery.co.uk

Offers a wide assortment of 1930s reproduction fabric, as well as adorable zakka-style lace zippers and trims. Ships from the United Kingdom.

Twiddletails
www.twiddletails.com

Offers an extensive range of 1930s reproduction fabrics, including beautifully curated bundles.

> Atsuko Matsuyama's fabric line is produced by Yuwa of Japan. Vintage feedsack and 1930s reproduction fabrics also work well for the projects in this book, including Old New 30s and Retro 30s by Lecien Fabrics of Japan. Atsuko Matsuyama's Original Sweet Fruit Handles are also produced by Lecien.

About the Author

Atsuko Matsuyama is one of Japan's leading quilt artists and fabric designers. In 1989, she opened her quilt studio A-Two. She often exhibits her work at the Tokyo International Quilt Festival and she makes regular television appearances.